Nocturnal Enuresis

Dedicated to Sue, Joe, Gregory and Luke

Nocturnal Enuresis
The child's experience

Richard J. Butler BSc, MSc, PhD, C Psychol, ABPsS
*Consultant Clinical Psychologist, Leeds Community and Mental Health
Trust, High Royds Hospital, Menston, Ilkley, West Yorkshire, UK
Honorary Lecturer, University of Leeds, UK*

Butterworth-Heinemann Ltd
Linacre House, Jordan Hill, Oxford OX2 8DP

R A member of the Reed Elsevier group plc

OXFORD LONDON BOSTON
MUNICH NEW DELHI SINGAPORE SYDNEY
TOKYO TORONTO WELLINGTON

First published 1994

©Butterworth-Heinemann Ltd 1994

_RJ476_
_.E6_
_B88_
_1994_

British Library Cataloguing in Publication Data

Butler, Richard J.
  Nocturnal Enuresis: The Child's Experience
  I. Title
  618.9263

  ISBN 0 7506 2132 X

Library of Congress Cataloguing in Publication Data

Butler, Richard J.
  Nocturnal enuresis: the child's experience/Richard J. Butler.
      p.   cm.
  Includes bibliographical references and index.
  ISBN 0 7506 2132 X
  1. Enuresis.   2. Enuresis – Psychological aspects.   3. Child
psychology.   I. Title.
RJ476.E6B88   94–32792
618.92'849–dc20   CIP

Printed in Great Britain by Biddles Ltd, Guildford and Kings Lynn

Contents

Preface

*'Children are the world's most valuable resource and
the greatest hope for the future'* John F. Kennedy

1987 saw the publication of 'Nocturnal Enuresis: Psychological Perspectives' which invited the consideration of enuresis within a psychological framework, in contrast to more traditional medical contentions. This thesis, founded on a particular model of psychology – personal construct theory – alluded naturally to the importance of the child's stance in debating the issues pertinent to nocturnal enuresis.

This view over recent years has emerged as apposite to the consideration of many childhood issues and has crystallized as increasingly significant in the field of nocturnal enuresis. The impetus for a shift towards the child's view as important is reinforced by perhaps the two most important debates on childhood issues that have surfaced in recent years. The Butler-Sloss Inquiry into Child Abuse in Cleveland recommended that: i. professionals should always listen carefully to what the child has to say and take seriously what is said, and ii. the views of and wishes of the child, particularly as to what should happen to him/her, should be taken into account by the professionals involved with their problems (Butler-Sloss, 1988).

The second source is Governmental and located in the Children's Act 1989 which takes as a central theme the requirement to acknowledge, take seriously and give due weight to the child's perspective in any decision making regarding the child (Stallard *et al.*, 1992).

Running alongside these pronouncements and of particular relevance to enuresis, is the accumulating evidence from our research which suggests that the way children and parents make sense of the problem determines the outcome of treatment. This theme became a fundamental thread in writing the book and gave rise to the title 'Nocturnal Enuresis: The child's experience' and with it the hope that readers both enrich their understanding of nocturnal enuresis and the child's stance towards it, and feel excited about their potential to assist children to successfully accomplish bladder control.

Richard Butler

Acknowledgements

I am indebted to the following colleagues for their encouragement, assistance, vision, counsel and wisdom in the development and refinement of this thesis. Amanda Pullan, Julie Kemp, Deborah Humphries and Marion Adams laboured unceasingly on the preparation of drafts and final manuscript; Shirley Robinson was a gem in ferreting out relevant literature; Susan Devlin my editor, assumed a welcome invitations mode which enabled the project to become an explorative venture; Anne Cotterill, Sean Davis and Brian Donovan provided forums which encouraged me to crystallize my thinking and express ideas; Penny Dobson, Director of E.R.I.C., whose energy and commitment to the cause provided the inspiration; Professor Denis Gill and Dr. Philip Hillard provided invaluable comments and suggestions; and Ed Redfern gave me the benefit of his statistical knowledge throughout the last 6 years of my research endeavours. The book owes much to the children and families with whom I have worked and I am grateful for their tolerance and patience.

Finally, I remain indebted beyond measure to Professor Don Bannister, who invited the exploration of meaning and who encouraged a propositional and child-focused approach to this problem. Sadly he died before I was able to share the ideas presented in this book. I wonder how he might have reacted?

*Besides the rivering waters of lither and thithering
waters of night!* James Joyce

1
The problem in context

Stop and think what the child might be going through.
Or try to imagine how you would feel if it was you who
had the enuresis trouble. Anon (1987)

Whilst at first nocturnal enuresis might be considered a fairly minor complaint, and in some contexts the source of a family joke, the problem assumes importance when observed from the child's perspective. Figure 1.1 illustrates the trauma of the child's experience. The perplexity, humiliation, alienation, verbal and physical abuse are all evident. So too are the inventive strategies children adopt to avoid discovery.

Many children go to great lengths to prevent others learning about their enuresis. However, a graphic description of coping with enuresis in a boarding school, where most events become public, is gallantly provided by a 16-year-old schoolgirl (Anon, 1987). Reflecting on the ordeal she described the following incidents:

- Feelings – anger, self-pity, moodiness, shame.
- Cognition – disappointment with self, perplexity.
- Behaviour – timid, unable to discuss, social isolation, withdrawing from school.
- Teachers' reactions – spray the room, shouted at, bawled at.
- Children's reactions – picked on, teased, made to feel different.

(Anon 1987)

Such experiences are far from unique. Nocturnal enuresis has been described by Collins (1980) as the most prevalent of all childhood problems, with estimates of a half to three-quarters of a million children over 7 years of age regularly suffering with bedwetting in Britain at any one time. In the USA the estimate is over 2 million children (Wagner and Hicks-Jimenez, 1986), and may be upwards of 7 million according to

Figure 1.1. The experience of bedwetting (From: *My enuresis*, Anon; *Nocturnal Enuresis: Psychological Perspectives*, Butler; personal communication, McClean).

Table 1.1. Prevalence rates (%) for nocturnal enuresis by sex from epidemiological surveys across different countries.

		5yrs	7yrs	9yrs	11yrs
Rutter *et al.* (1973) G.B	boys	13.4	21.9	9	–
	girls	13.9	15.5	5.6	–
Verhulst *et al.* (1985) Holland	boys	17	15	9	9
	girls	9	7	7	2
Feehan *et al.* (1990) New Zealand	boys	19	16	9	9
	girls	15	14	9	4
Devlin (1991) Ireland	boys	17	16	13	11
	girls	16	13	10	8

Definition: at least one wetting episode per month.

Scharf and Jennings (1988). Although by no means all of these children are brought to the attention of the medical services – Novello and Novello (1987) suggest less than half are seen by GPs and paediatricians – nocturnal enuresis remains one of the most frequent problems faced by health workers. The clinical time and demand expected of child health workers in this field is inexhaustible.

The problem is also persistent. Epidemiological surveys suggest 13–19% of boys and 9–16% girls at 5 years of age wet the bed at least once per month (Table 1.1), with a steady decline during the childhood years and adolescence but with 2–3% still wetting with regularity during late teens and early adulthood (Forsythe and Redmond, 1974; Pierce, 1980). Scharf and Jennings (1988) reflect on the size of the problem in early adulthood by noting both British and American studies of naval recruits show that bedwetting is the main cause of military service rejection.

Verhulst *et al.*'s (1985) survey, depicted in Fig. 1.2 illustrates:

- The rate of decline with the child's age, which Forsythe and Redmond (1974) calculated as between 14% for 5 to 9-year-olds and 16% for those 10–18 years old. So about 1 in every 7 or 8 children will 'outgrow' the problem or develop nocturnal bladder control each year if no treatment is advocated.
- However by no means will all children 'grow out of it', and

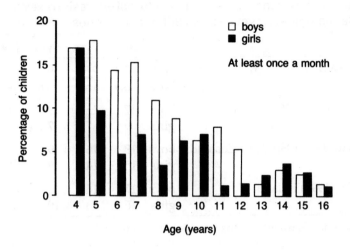

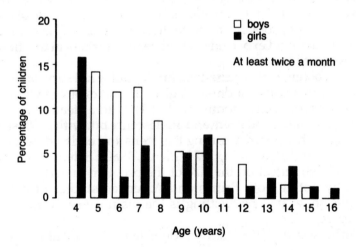

Figure 1.2. The prevalence of bedwetting by age and sex with a minimum of one and two wetting episodes a month. (Reproduced with permission from Verhulst *et al.*, 1985.)

with *no* valid predictors of which children will become dry spontaneously (Doleys, 1977), nocturnal enuresis can be construed as one of the most *chronic* childhood problems.

- Not until the eighth year are the number of boys achieving bladder control equal to the number of girls becoming dry in the fifth year. During childhood (5–12 years) boys are much more likely to experience bedwetting than girls, yet during adolescence the rate evens out.
- The rate of decline is less smooth and regular for girls compared with boys. Devlin (1991) found an almost identical pattern in a survey of Irish children. There are rises or peaks at ages 7, 10 and 14 whether Verhulst *et al.*'s (1985) definition of at least one, or at least two wetting episodes a month are taken. This indicates a more complicated picture for girls, with secondary enuresis, urinary tract infection, puberty and possibly sexual abuse all potentially influencing the uneven rate of nocturnal bladder acquisition.

Although epidemiology surveys tend to opt for generous criteria such as one or more wetting episodes per month, most children seen clinically will be wetting indisputably more frequently. Some children may be bedwetting with a frequency of up to 3 or 4 times per night. A consensus of opinion suggests about half bedwetting children are regular wetters, i.e. more than once per week (Verhulst *et al.*, 1985) but only a few (15%) will wet every night (Foxman *et al.*, 1986).

Whilst frequency of bedwetting has been employed to define enuresis in population surveys, this variable is less than evident in most clinical working definitions of enuresis. Nocturnal enuresis has been defined as:

> an involuntary discharge of urine by day or night, or both, in the absence of congenital or acquired defects of the CNS or urinary tract in a child aged 5 or over (Forsythe and Butler, 1989).

Selection of such a definition *excludes*:

- Voluntary discharge of urine – acts of wilful micturition such as urination into fish tanks, cavity walls or gouged out holes in the mattress. However, it does not exclude urination in unusual situations such as a wardrobe when the child remains asleep and 'dreams he is at the toilet'.

- Bedwetting due to urological or neurological pathology or abnormality. Such instances might include impairment of renal function, overt neurological disease, or bladder outflow obstruction (Whiteside and Arnold, 1975). The exclusion of organic causes refines a central tenet in the definition of nocturnal enuresis by divorcing it from incontinence. The two should *not* be used interchangeably, with incontinence reserved for involuntary wetting with an organic aetiology.
- Children younger than 5 years of age. The choice of an age point is somewhat arbitrary but reflects the natural course of bladder acquisition. Verhulst *et al.* (1985) and Cohen (1975) have argued for flexibility in age criteria due to the different rates of acquisition for boys and girls. Extrapolation from Verhulst *et al.*'s (1985) figures suggests that not until the eighth year is the prevalence rate for boys equivalent to that for girls at 5 years and thus age 8 would logically set the criteria for boys.

The debate is further confused by Shaffer's (1980) contention that children who wet after 4 years of age have significantly *less* chance of becoming dry at night during the following year than a child of 2 or 3 who continues to wet. Thus children wetting at 4 years of age might be described as having more of an entrenched or chronic problem. The probability of becoming dry thereafter remains even lower, as Rutter *et al.* (1973) demonstrated only 1.5% of 5-year-old bedwetters became dry in the following 2 years.

A fundamental part of the equation in decisions regarding the provision of a service is the parental and child concerns and anxieties about nocturnal enuresis. Paradoxically, much child work is focused on parental fears and desperation about children they perceive as failing to develop normally, behaving inappropriately or suffering emotionally. Brazelton (1973) and Butler (1987) have suggested bedwetting becomes a problem at the point where parental concern is expressed. The age varies enormously and the reasons for parental concern are widespread, yet fear over emotional consequences for the child and parental exasperation and developing intolerance are clear markers that should trigger our concern for the child and family.

Intolerance and impatience can lead parents towards punitive reactions. Many writers have articulated the harrowing ordeals children have endured because of their bedwetting. Rowe (1987) reported a child wrapped in wet sheets and made to stand in the cold; Warady *et al.* (1991) observed incidents of a child with enuresis being forced to sleep in a chicken coop and another in a bathtub; Baller (1975) made note of a child being made to sleep on uncovered bedsprings in the garage, whilst Smith (1974) recounted a child who had been burned

Table 1.2. Some stark reminders of how children have been 'treated' in the past, under the guise of therapy.
Sources: Glicklich (1951); Mowrer and Mowrer (1938); Gorodzinsky (1984).

Punishment	*Medicine/potions*
Rubbing child's face in wet sheet	Testicle of hedgehog
Pour ashes over the head	Juniper berries
Beatings	Belladonna
Force child to drink own urine	Desiccated hog's bladder
Ridicule	Swine urine
Burned and threatened	Powdered trachea of cock
Wear wet pyjamas around neck	Claws of goat
Blister the buttocks	Injection of saline
	Injection of paraffin
	Tea of chrysanthemum
	Gastric mucosa of hens
Aids to waking/avoiding deep sleep	*Prevention of urination*
Cold water	Penile bandages
Blasts of air	Sealing or constriction of
Awaken in 2nd hour of sleep	urinary orifice
Sleep on hard mattress	Local freezing of the external
Attach steel spikes to child's back	genitalia
Tie a cotton reel over the spine	
Sleep on golf balls	
	Surgery
	Cauterization of the uretha
	Circumcision

with a hot poker and threatened with further mutilation for continued wetting. Schaefer (1979) brought attention to other extreme parental reactions including beating, ridiculing in front of peers, forcing the child to drink his own urine and wearing wet pyjamas around the neck. Such acts of desperation illustrate the frustrations and impotence parents often feel when faced with their child's persistent bedwetting.

Children with enuresis have also been subjected to a catalogue of misguided 'treatments' designed to keep the child awake or reduce the flow of urine. Table 1.2 highlights some of the barbaric attempts which now, thankfully, reside only in history texts.

With the abandonment of such techniques, a child may still, however, feel intimidated and anxious in the modern day clinic, particularly when told 'you'll grow out of it' or handed an 'electric box' (an enuresis alarm) to put on the bed and told without explanation that such apparatus will stop the bedwetting.

Children with enuresis deserve more. The following chapters explore the problem of enuresis taking, as fundamental, the child's perspective. With this arises the view that by engaging children in the process of assessment and choice of treatment the means of delivering effective services is enhanced.

2

Bladder functioning

*Science is what you know. Philosophy is what you
don't know.* Bertrand Russell

An appreciation of the bladder's physiological functioning and
maturation will assist the therapist in devising appropriate
treatment interventions and communicate an understanding to
child and parent.

Figure 2.1 illustrates some examples of children's understanding of the bladder, which essentially improves with age
and biology lessons. A fragile looking 'bag' with or without
'tubes' leading to and from all manner of places is the standard
impression of those under 10 years of age. At 11 and 12 years
the idea of the bladder as a reservoir is acknowledged, but
notions of how the bladder remains watertight are as yet not
considered. Friman and Warzak (1990) describe the bladder as
an elastic, viscous organ with a complex arrangement of
smooth muscle, blood vessels and connective tissue. Figure 2.2
presents an illustration of the bladder structure.

Norgaard *et al.* (1989) suggest the daytime bladder functioning (of bed wetters) is similar to non-enuretic children. The
cycle of normal bladder functioning has been described by
Fielding (1982) and essentially consists of filling, storage, desire
to void, postponement of urination and micturition.

Filling

The body of the bladder, known as the detrusor muscles,
remains relaxed when the bladder is empty, whilst pelvic floor
muscles contract to ensure the urethra remains closed.

By peristalsis urine is transported from the kidneys through
the ureters to the bladder. It fills at approximately 1 ml/min
(Shaffer, 1980), yet normally during the night the rate of urine

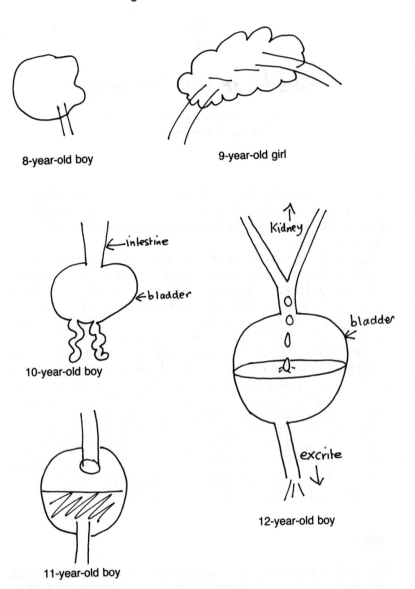

Figure 2.1. Children's notions about the structure of the bladder.

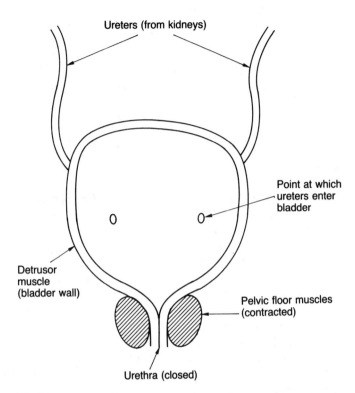

Figure 2.2. Diagrammatic representation of the structure of the bladder – frontal section.

production decreases to around a half of usual daytime production (Norgaard, 1992). This is the result of a release of plasma arginine vasopressin (AVP) which reduces the production and increases the osmolality of urine (Norgaard *et al.*, 1989). With less urine produced the bladder capacity is normally not reached and therefore the need to void during the night is not experienced.

Some evidence suggests that children with enuresis may not produce AVP and thus high volumes of urine, of a less concentrated nature, are produced at night-time (Norgaard *et al.*, 1989; Wood *et al.*, 1994). This means the bladder capacity may be exceeded with the need to void during the night as a consequence.

As the bladder fills, the detrusor muscles of the bladder wall relax and expand, so the volume of urine within the bladder increases without the internal pressure rising inordinately. Norgaard (1992) found that, as with non-enuretic children, the bladder wall of most children with enuresis does not contract with filling. Where there are contractions the condition is known as an *unstable bladder*, and Norgaard (1992) argues this is rare with children who demonstrate night-only wetting.

Storage

The efficiency of the bladder to store urine depends upon both the distensibility of the detrusor muscles and the capacity for 'water tightness'. The bladder adapts to the increasing volumes of urine because of the elastic properties of the smooth muscle and collagen of the detrusor muscle (Varni, 1983). Simultaneously, the bladder prevents 'leakage' through the urethra by a combination of muscular actions, involving the *internal ure-thral orifice* located at the bladder neck, a thickening of smooth muscle fibres under voluntary control; the *external urethral sphincter*, composed of striated muscle and capable of maintaining tone over long periods of time (Gosling *et al.*, 1981) and contractions of the pelvic floor muscles which pushes the urethra upwards.

As Fig. 2.3 illustrates, the bladder capacity, or amount of urine the child can hold, develops with age. At 3 years of age the capacity is about 5 fl oz and at 6 years about 8 fl oz with a linear correlation between age and bladder capacity from birth to 11 years. After 12 years the capacity remains stable at approximately 15–20 fl oz.

Bladder capacity is functional rather than structural, and varies between individuals, with children with enuresis tending not to be able to hold as much as other children (Fielding, 1980) which possibly leads to a more frequent need to toilet. Troup and Hodgson (1971) found that when passively filled under anaesthesia the bladder volume was normal with enuretic children. Thus children with enuresis may have difficulty in tolerating large volumes and are more likely to have bladder contractions 'early' leading to *small functional bladder capacity*.

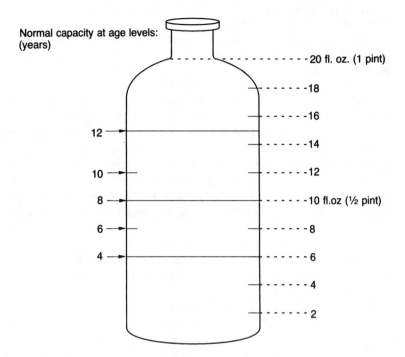

Figure 2.3. The development of bladder capacity with age, illustrated by means of milk bottle volume. 1 fluid ounce=28,41 ml. Formula for assessing bladder capacity: capacity (in fluid ounces)=age in years +2 (Berger *et al.*, 1983).

> Functional bladder capacity = the volume at which there is a strong desire to void

Desire to void

At the point when the bladder begins to reach the functional capacity, the detrusor muscles, in response to increased stretching and tension, begin waves of contractions. This is signalled to the higher cortical centres of the brain and normally perceived as a sensation of fullness, the need to go, or urgency. Other stimuli incidentally can also provoke the desire to void including bacterial irritation, the sound of running water, the sight of a toilet or anxiety.

For some children the urge to void may occur without warning (Fielding, 1982) and the bladder contractions may give rise to reflux – the backward passage of urine up the ureters – increasing the risk of urinary infection.

The signal of bladder fullness may compete for recognition amongst a host of other stimuli. During the day a child engrossed in play may not become aware of the sensations of fullness until very late (having to dash to the toilet) or not at all (with a wetting episode the result). During sleep the perception of signals from the detrusor muscles necessitates an appropriate response if the child is to remain dry. Fielding (1982) suggests bedwetting children may fail to react appropriately to such signals because of:

- perceptual insensitivity – a failure to recognise the signal;
- perceptual incomprehension – a failure to recognise the meaning of the signal;
- perceptual distractibility – a failure to detect the signal from amongst a number of other signals.

Postponement

The bladder's capacity to postpone urination once the detrusor muscles begin contracting may be achieved at first without the child's awareness. Fielding (1982) has described daytime movements or posture, such as crouching, crossing the legs, or compressing the thighs which induces the bladder neck to lift and postpone urination. During sleep, similar body movements may occur just prior to urination (Broughton, 1968). Signals from the body movements may act as additional signals to those from the bladder, and a failure to detect the combination of both results in bedwetting.

Once the desire to void has been perceived, the urge can be suppressed voluntarily, whereby the child 'holds' urine in the bladder by tensing the muscles of the pelvic floor, keeping the bladder outlet closed. During artificial filling of the bladder whilst asleep, Norgaard (1989a) discovered wetting was avoided by the contraction of pelvic floor muscles, but wetting occurred when the pelvic floor muscles failed to contract. Thus detrusor contractions appear to be suppressed by contractions of the pelvic floor. Immediate recognition of bladder signals enables postponement until a toilet is reached; delayed recognition leads to the child having difficulty in holding and needing to 'dash' to the toilet; whilst lack of awareness of the signals inevitably leads to urination.

Micturition

Stretch receptors in the bladder wall are stimulated when the bladder capacity is reached. This causes the bladder neck to descend and reflexive contractions of the detrusor opens the sphincter to allow urine to emerge from the urethra under pressure.

Voided volume = total volume expelled via urethra

Vis Melsen (1992) noted four types of flow pattern with bedwetting children.

- Sharp peak. ⎫
- Biphasic (2 peaks). ⎬ normal
- Saw tooth (many peaks). ⎫
- Flat (no peaks). ⎬ abnormal

Most children have a normal pattern of micturition. However, some children, notably those with associated daytime wetting, may not completely empty the bladder due to contractions of the external sphincter when it ought to be relaxed (Berger *et al.*, 1983).

Nocturnal bladder control is typically the final achievement in a developmental sequence (Stein and Susser, 1967a) where bowel control during sleep marks the beginning, followed by bowel control during waking hours. Bladder control during the day soon follows, and following a variable interval, night-time control of the bladder is established.

However, some children will achieve dryness at night before

accomplishing daytime bladder control. In a sample of 2600 children Jarvelin *et al.* (1988) found that with enuretic children 65% had night only wetting, 20% daytime wetting and 15% both day and night wetting. Perhaps the indications are that diurnal and nocturnal bladder control may not be governed by the same factors (Fielding, 1982). In a longitudinal study of children in New Zealand Fergusson *et al.* (1986) discovered 7.5% of children were reportedly achieving dry nights by age 2; 57% at age 3; and 81% at 4 years of age, suggesting normal development of bladder control occurs around the third year, with evidently some individual variability. The following sequence can be presented as a guide to normal development:

- birth–6 months   bladder emptying occurs frequently during the day and night, as a *reflex* action.
- 6–12 months   bladder emptying is less frequent due to CNS *inhibition* of the reflex action.
- 1–2 years   child consciously *perceives* bladder fullness and begins to communicate this behaviourally and verbally.
- 3–4 years   awareness of bladder fullness increases and child develops the ability to *postpone* urination.
- 4–5 years   the ability to *consciously control voiding* continues to develop until the child can control voiding at any degree of fullness, and on command.

Warady *et al.* (1991)

An explanation of bladder functioning for the child is imperative. Depending upon the child's age the following suggestions usually prove adequate:

- Consider the bladder is *a bag of muscle*.
- It adjusts, or *expands* as the amount of urine (waste water) collects.
- When *full*, and the bladder cannot expand any further, the bladder walls begin to *contract* and this is sent as a message to the brain.
- During the day this contraction is *sensed* as a need to use the toilet and sometimes as *urgency*.

- During sleep the message (contraction) is difficult to decode or understand, and when the bladder cannot hold any longer, it begins to empty.
- To stay dry the message has to be decoded and the body react to the bladder contractions by:

    (i) keeping the bladder muscles around the outlet tightly closed, like having to *hold* until a toilet is found during the day. Thus you learn to sleep through the night by being able to hold on.

    or

    (ii) waking up to use the toilet.

- Both holding or waking to a full bladder are difficult skills to master and it is, therefore, quite amazing that so many children do indeed achieve it.

3

Biological beliefs about bedwetting

A powerful idea communicates some of its strength to him who challenges it. Marcel Proust

The unremitting search for an explanation for nocturnal enuresis has unlocked a range of avenues of enquiry. Some vistas have proved extremely fruitful whilst others – notably psychoanalytic models – have withered and all but died. A crude

Table 3.1. Children's beliefs about biological causes for their enuresis (*n* = 50 children).

Reason	Mean rating (0–6 Scale)	How controllable (%)	How unstable (%)
Organic pathology • a physical problem	2.52	0	50
Urinary tract infection • urine infection/painful urination	2.02	11	72
Nocturnal polyuria • I make too much urine	2.65	5	25
Small FBC • I can't hold enough urine	2.50	0	38
Dysfunctional detrusor activity • my bladder doesn't work properly	3.86	3	21
Disturbance of the arousal system • I sleep too deeply	4.62	5	29
Genetic predisposition • It runs in the family	1.76	0	38
Maturational lag • my bladder is not fully developed yet	2.73	0	16

distinction may be made to separate biological and psychological theories, the former of which becomes the focus of this chapter. Biological notions suggest enuresis arises as a consequence of:

- organic pathology;
- urinary tract infection;
- nocturnal polyuria;
- small functional bladder capacity;
- dysfunctional detrusor activity;
- disturbance of the arousal system;
- genetic predisposition;
- maturational lag.

Children's ideas about the aetiology of their enuresis are presented in Table 3.1. Fifty children were asked to rate each statement on a 0–6 Likert Scale according to how strongly they felt they were reasons for bedwetting.

When statements were given a high rating (4, 5 or 6 on the scale), children were invited to remark on the controllability and stability of the cause as in the following example:

Reasons for bedwetting	Stability		Controllabiliy	
	Stable stays the same	Unstable changes from day to day	Control I can control	No control I can't control
1 Deep sleep	✓			✓
2 runs in the family	✓			✓
3 I can't hold enough		✓		✓

Here a child has provided three strong reasons (rated 4 or above) for their bedwetting. The example indicates that he believes 'deep sleep' and 'runs in the family' are both stable and uncontrollable events, whilst 'I can't hold enough' is construed to be unstable yet also uncontrollable.

Perceived controllability and stability were measured as a percentage of responses and presented in Table 3.1. Depth of sleep is strongly perceived to be a cause of bedwetting. Children wholeheartedly subscribe to the idea that biological causes are not controllable, yet interestingly they view some causes, notably urinary tract infection and physical problems as changeable or unstable.

Organic pathology

Given the definition of nocturnal enuresis in Chapter 1, which excludes children with urological or neurological causes for their enuresis, this explanation might promptly be dismissed. However, Cohen (1975) and Schmitt (1990) both suggest some 3% of bedwetting children seen in paediatric settings may have an organic basis for the condition. As Schmitt (1990) emphasizes, differential diagnosis assumes a major importance when treatment options are considered. Problems such as obstructive uropathy, neurogenic bladder and developmental anomalies of the urinary tract remain the perogative of paediatric surgeons and urologists.

Concern for such organic causes is alerted when there is:

- constant wetness (dampness);
- abnormal urine flow (e.g. dribbling, difficulty starting);
- change in gait.

Breugelmans and Wyndaele (1992) found the more symptoms (such as frequency, urgency, daytime wetting) a child complained of, the greater the need for urodynamic investigations to screen for bladder instability, bladder pathology and minor spina bifida. Weider and Hauri (1985) have proposed that a blocked nose, snoring or sleep apnoea (stopping breathing) may lead to bedwetting, and they recommend adenoidectomy, to help remedy the problem. Medical conditions giving rise to wetting include diabetes mellitus – which is excluded with the absence of sugar in the urinalysis – and diabetes insipidus, which is excluded when the specific gravity of urine exceeds 1015 (Schmitt, 1990). For many children the surgery or clinic can prove a threatening situation, with expectations of physical examinations, and injections. If it is suggested and explained that there is no physical reason for the wetting and no investigative procedure or blood taking will occur, a welcome sense of relief and reassurance is evident.

Urinary tract infection (UTI)

A urine culture is indicated where symptoms of UTI are present: These include:

- intermittent daytime wetting;
- painful/stinging urination;
- urine with a foul odour.

UTI is fairly common amongst young children. Some 1% of 5-year-old girls suffer according to Savage *et al.* (1969), and children with nocturnal enuresis are five times more likely to have UTI than other children.

Children most susceptible to UTI appear to be:

- Girls. Dodge *et al.* (1970) found 10% of girls in a bedwetting population had UTI.
- Those with a greater frequency of wetting accidents.
- Children wetting by day and night (Jarvelin *et al.*, 1991).

A number of researchers have demonstrated that clearing up the UTI often does not reduce bedwetting (e.g. Zaleski *et al.*, 1973) which suggests the infection is not a cause of enuresis but possibly a consequence of it, as bedwetting may facilitate the ascent of pathogenic organisms to the bladder (Shaffer, 1980). Whilst remaining largely uncontrollable, some 11% of children (Table 3.1) believe they have a degree of control over UTI as a cause of enuresis. UTI is also regarded by children as the most unstable of all biological causes. This then presents an opportunity for involving children in discussing what options there are for asserting more control through identifying what produces or generates the instability – for example not wiping themselves properly, wearing damp underclothes, not drinking sufficient fluids, or not completely emptying the bladder on toilet visits. Engaging children in such discussion can enable them to bring about change - self generated change – through awareness.

Nocturnal polyuria (production of excessive urine)

This explanation localizes the problem in the kidneys. The suggestion is that bedwetting is a consequence of the kidneys failing to concentrate urine during sleep, resulting in nocturnal urine production which exceeds the bladder's capacity. Many mothers believe their children produce excessive amounts of urine, although this is not the most prevalent of beliefs amongst children (Table 3.1).

Normally production of the hormone arginine vasopressin (AVP) in the hypothalamus (and storage in the posterior lobe of the pituitary gland) with release during sleep, causes the kidneys to concentrate urine by reabsorption of water through the distal tubes of the kidney (Hladky and Rink, 1986). Thus urine production during sleep is significantly less than during the waking hours.

Evidence for a lack of AVP release with bedwetting children is suggested by:

- an excess in volume of urine produced at night compared with the day (Norgaard, Pederson and Djurhuus, 1985);
- a lack of production of AVP at night compared with the day (Norgaard, et al., 1989);
- a lack of production of AVP at night compared with non-enuretic children (Rittig et al., 1989);
- a lack of concentration of urine (osmolality) during the night compared with non-enuretic children (Rittig et al., 1989)

Holland et al. (in preparation) have suggested that a disorder of AVP storage, transport or secretion, with reduced amount of hormone released, might either be genetically determined or the result of psychosocial deprivation in the same way that growth hormone release from the pituitary gland is suppressed under certain socially disadvantaged situations (e.g. Powell et al., 1967).

However, questions remain over the AVP hypothesis as a causal factor for all children with nocturnal enuresis. There is uneasiness around the following issues:

- Not all children with nocturnal enuresis fail to produce AVP at night, and thus the nocturnal polyuria theory assumes selectivity in accounting for only a percentage of children's bedwetting.

- Achieving dry nights may be dependent upon the child's ability to respond appropriately to bladder contractions (through waking or holding), irrespective of how much urine is produced.
- It remains unclear whether children who become dry spontaneously (approximately 15% per year) or those who respond successfully to conditioning treatment (about 70%) do so by developing a normal circadian rhythm of AVP or by developing a greater awareness of bladder sensations.

Small functional bladder capacity

A popular formulation, elaborated by Starfield (1967), is that children with nocturnal enuresis have comparatively smaller functional bladder capacities, which prevents the child being able to hold all the urine produced during the night. A *functional* rather than structural difference is emphasized by Troup and Hodgson (1971) as they discovered the structural capacity of the bladder is similar with both bedwetting and non-bedwetting children.

Functional bladder capacity (fbc) is defined as: 'the volume of urine voided after the child has postponed micturition for as long as possible' Houts (1991)

Fbc can be measured with a graduated container in the following ways:

- The larger of two voidings after drinking copious volumes of fluid and holding for as long as possible (Starfield, 1967; Fielding, 1980).
- The average of all voidings over a 24-hour period (Troup and Hodgson, 1971).
- The average of all voidings in 1 week (Zaleski *et al.*, 1973).

Good indications of small fbc include:

- daytime urgency to use the toilet (Fielding, 1980);
- frequent micturition of small quantities during the day (Esperanca and Gerrard, 1969a);
- frequent night-time wetting episodes (Novello and Novello, 1987);
- wetting both by day and night (Zaleski *et al.*, 1973; Jarvelin *et al.*, 1991).

The hypothesis suggesting that nocturnal enuresis results from small fbc arose from studies in the late 1960s and early 1970s (Esperanca and Gerrard, 1969a; Starfield and Mellits, 1968; Zaleski *et al.*, 1973). More recently, the view being adopted is that small fbc may be a *correlate* or indeed, a *consequence*, rather than a cause of enuresis (Houts, 1991). This position is supported by:

- The considerable overlap in fbc between bedwetting and non-bedwetting children (Troup and Hodgson, 1971), suggesting small fbc cannot account for *all* children with enuresis.
- An increase in fbc is *not* a prerequisite condition for the attainment of dryness, particularly for children who wet only at night (Fielding, 1980).
- For day and night wetting children, increases in fbc appear to arise *after* the achievement of dryness (Fielding, 1980).
- Artificial filling of the bladder during sleep causes non-bedwetting children to wake, yet produces urination in children with enuresis (Sorotzkin, 1984), suggesting the bladder capacity is less of a determinant than how bladder contractions are perceived and reacted to by the child.

Dysfunctional detrusor activity (unstable bladder)

The belief that enuresis is caused by a malfunctioning bladder is reasonably common amongst children (Table 3.1). Houts (1991) has summarized the evidence suggesting bedwetting results from spontaneous detrusor contractions during sleep occurring at lower than normal pressures, leading to spontaneous voiding with low bladder volumes. This, argues Houts, is unlikely, however, to have an organic cause in most enuretic children, but rather may be the result of a lack of coordination between the muscles involved in voiding.

As discussed in Chapter 2, on voiding, the pelvic floor muscles normally relax to produce a peak rate of urine flow. Sometimes *dyssynergia* (pelvic floor contractions during voiding) occurs, resulting in a weak stream, stopping and starting, and incomplete emptying of the bladder. This may subsequently lead to UTI, day wetting, urgency, frequency and low fbc.

However, Norgaard *et al.* (1989) failed to discover such dyssynergic activity during day or night with night-only bed wetters, suggesting it is not a causative factor in uncomplicated enuresis.

Nevertheless, Houts (1991) claims the extensive work undertaken by Norgaard (1989a, 1989b) suggests the avoidance of night-time wetting occurs when children prevent detrusor contractions by spontaneously contracting the pelvic floor muscles, but wetting occurs if the pelvic floor muscles fail to contract and respond in the same way as they do with normal daytime voiding, by relaxing. Thus the predicament for bedwetting children is to acquire or learn the opposite pelvic floor muscle response (*contraction*) in response to bladder contractions, to that which occurs during daytime voiding (*relaxation* of the pelvic floor muscles). Houts (1991) proposes that one mechanism of action with urine alarm treatments may be the conditioning of pelvic floor contractions in response to bladder sensations of fullness.

What is suggested by the discussion of biological explanations is that far from being considered a unitary problem, nocturnal enuresis might best be thought of as a group of conditions with differing aetiologies. Table 3.2 summarizes the child's experiences of 'biological' symptoms and the relationship to possible causes.

The arousal system (deep sleep)

The deep sleep theory appears to make eminent logical sense. Of all explanations surveyed it is seen by children, by some margin, as the most likely cause of nocturnal enuresis (Butler *et al.*, 1994). As Table 3.1 shows it is also regarded as uncontrollable and relatively stable, and thus something children feel they can do little about. Deep sleep is also the most heavily

Table 3.2. The child's experience of bladder functioning and relationship to types of problem

• constantly wet or damp	
• abnormal urine flow	→ possible organic cause
(dribbling, difficulty starting)	
• daytime wetting	
• painful urination	→ urinary tract infection
• urine with foul (fishy) odour	
• dilute (not concentrated) urine	→ nocturnal polyuria/
• excessive amounts of urine	lack of ADH secretion
(at night)	
• urgency in the daytime	
• frequent micturition of small volumes	→ small bladder capacity
• frequent night-time accidents	
• wet by day and night	
• weak urine flow	
• stopping and starting of urinary flow	→ unstable bladder
• incomplete bladder emptying	(dysfunctional detrusor)

endorsed view of mothers (Haque *et al.*, 1981; Butler *et al.*, 1986; Butler and Brewin 1986) who experience the difficulty of waking their enuretic children to toilet at night.

Boyd (1960), however, discovered children who did not wet the bed were as difficult to arouse from sleep as bedwetting children. Parents may have little, or no, reason to wake a non-bedwetting sibling, and therefore underestimate the difficulty of arousing children from sleep.

Graham (1973) points out that difficulty of arousal may not be related to depth of sleep, but may, for example, be associated with other consequences faced by the bedwetting child – such unpleasant repercussions as parental disapproval, changing wet sheets and becoming cold. Figure 3.1 illustrates the nature of sleep, measured by EEG. It consists of non-REM sleep with four stages of progressively deeper sleep through which the child moves before emerging again into lighter stages of sleep. This cyclical pattern continues throughout the night. Stages 3 and 4 tend to dominate non-REM sleep during the first part of the night (Pressman, 1986), with cycles lasting about 70–90 minutes. REM (Rapid Eye Movement) sleep is qualitatively different sleep with the muscles of the body paralysed and

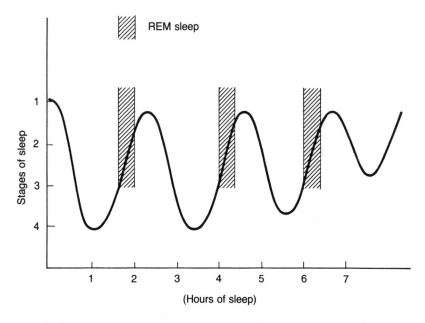

Figure 3.1. The nature of sleep measured by EEG: non-REM sleep has four stages (From Butler, 1987).

dreams predominating. Interestingly, very few enuretic episodes are recorded during REM sleep (Ritvo *et al.*, 1969; Scharf and Jennings, 1988).

A gathering body of evidence has accumulated against enuresis being a result of deep sleep. The evidence includes:

- Enuretic episodes occur during all stages of sleep, in proportion to the amount of time spent in that stage (Kales *et al.*, 1977; Mikkelson *et al.*, 1980; Norgaard, Hansen and Neilsen, 1985)
- With a little variance (bedwetting boys having marginally less stage 4 sleep than non-enuretic boys), the sleep pattern of all children remains similar (Gillin *et al.*, 1982)
- No difference in sleep patterns of bedwetting children between those nights they have enuretic episodes and those nights they remain dry (Gillin *et al.*, 1982).

Conveying such information to children proves illuminating. It is important to propose that:

- bedwetting is not a result of deep sleep;
- bedwetting is more likely to result from a failure to respond to bladder signals;
- when bladder signals assume importance, the child will develop control through holding (contracting pelvic floor muscles) *or* waking;
- children do wake to important signals (such as illness, unusual noises) and sleep through unimportant signals (such as the noise of traffic).

Genetic predisposition

Through many of the families of bedwetting children runs a history of nocturnal enuresis (Devlin, 1991). Bakwin (1971) and Jarvelin *et al.* (1988) found that where both parents had themselves been enuretic during childhood, the risk of enuresis was high, with a 77% chance that their child would have nocturnal enuresis. With only one parent enuretic as a child, the risk was 43%, and where neither parent suffered in childhood, the child had only a 15% chance of being a bedwetter.

Further evidence of the link was found in Fergusson *et al.*'s (1986) longitudinal study, where age of attaining bladder control was strongly determined by family history of enuresis. Jarvelin *et al.* (1991) also recently found parental history of enuresis was strongly related to the presence of wetting with both night only wetters and night and day wetters.

Such evidence of family history has stimulated the search for a genetic link, through twin study methodology. Bakwin (1971) found that with boys, 70% of monozygotic (mz) twins (i.e. twins of identical genetic make-up) were concordant for nocturnal enuresis, compared with 31% of dizygotic twin (dz) boys (i.e. twins with a different genetic make-up). Interestingly, although the same trend was observed with girls (65% of mz twins concordant compared with 44% of dz twins), the difference was not statistically significant. Thus, although a reasonably strong genetic link is demonstrated with boys, this is less clear with girls.

An autosomal (non sex linked) dominant gene with reduced penetrance has been the genetic model favoured by geneticists (Lunt, personal communication). However, as with most theoretical concepts, some aspects remain indefinite:

- The *mode of action*: this has been suggested to be one where bladder vulnerability (e.g. capacity, instability) is genetically determined (Taylor and Turner, 1975), yet other workers suggest that the production and release of AVP (arginine vasopressin) by the hypothalamus and pituitary glands may be what is influenced genetically (Holland *et al.* in preparation).
- The *concept of vulnerability*: twin studies suggest a high level of concordance for enuresis with mz twins (Bakwin, 1971). However, some mz twin members (30% of boys) and a quarter of children where both parents were enuretic in childhood, both of whom would seem especially vulnerable to enuresis, do indeed achieve bladder control. What, therefore, enables such vulnerable children to avoid becoming enuretic would be an interesting and important area of study.

The penetrance model, proposed by geneticists, implies the child inherits a *vulnerability* to enuresis. Whether such a child becomes enuretic or not may be influenced by environmental factors such as stress, parental expectation or social circumstances.

- The question regarding *mechanism of transfer*: here the issue concerns how the vulnerability to enuresis is 'passed on' from parent to child. The mode may be environmental, as proposed by Butler (1987) where parents who were themselves enuretic as children, treat their children differently to parents who were not enuretic. Such parents may show greater tolerance for bedwetting, and adopt attitudes and expectations which are conducive to continued bedwetting. One such expectation might be that their child will 'grow out of it', as they themselves had done. This might result in delayed interventions such as toilet training, which Fergusson *et al.* (1986) found related to delayed attainment of bladder control.

Gathering a 'family tree' during interviews with the parents and locating individuals who were bedwetting beyond 5 years, may prove intriguing for the child. They:

- may discover, for the first time, that a parent experienced the very same problem – a knowledge which might unite the pair in developing strategies to overcome the bedwetting;
- can understand that bladder control may be the result of inherited tendencies, such as hair or eye colour, and are not, therefore, to be blamed for the bedwetting;
- may realize their own children in turn could experience the same difficulty, and as suggested by Morgan (1984), may promise to act sympathetically and supportively towards them.

Maturational lag

It has been argued that the achievement of bladder control occurs with the completion of physiological maturity and is independent of training (Crosby, 1950), and thus by contrast, delayed maturation of bladder functioning would lead to continued bedwetting. The theory of maturational lag can only be an explanation of persistent bedwetting and must exempt children with onset or secondary enuresis for their period of dryness presumably demonstrates a maturity of physiological structures.

Evidence for maturational delay as a causative factor comes from a variety of sources:

- Signs of delayed maturation in bedwetting children compared with non-bedwetters:

  - lower birth weight (Jarvelin et al., 1988);
  - shorter in height (Essen and Peckham, 1976; Jarvelin et al., 1991);
  - 'soft signs' of neurological delay, such as clumsiness, fine motor coordination and perceptual dysfunction (Jarvelin, 1989).

- The increase in prevalence amongst boys suggests a maturational lag according to Friman and Warzak (1990) as boys are generally slower on developmental measures compared with girls.

- The longitudinal study of Fergusson *et al.* (1986) indicated that measures of delayed motor development were associated with delays in attaining bladder control.
- Evidence of 'immature' EEG records with persistent bedwetters (Salmon *et al.*, 1973).

Both Jarvelin (1989) and Fergusson *et al.* (1990) have proposed a similar model to account for primary and secondary enuresis, suggesting they represent 'two sides of the same coin'. Thus on the one hand the child's capacity to acquire and maintain nocturnal bladder control is related to the rate of maturation of the physiological mechanisms – a failure resulting in primary enuresis. On the other hand, a developmentally 'frail' child may be more vulnerable in stressful situations and thus be susceptible to relapsing or developing secondary or onset enuresis.

Delayed maturation *per se* may only account for a small number of children with nocturnal enuresis because the capacity to achieve dryness (if only temporarily) before the age of 5 years has been shown in a number of ways:

- Clinical interventions by Brazelton (1962) indicated 98.5% of 5-year-olds could become dry.
- Fergusson *et al.* (1986) showed only 11% of children had not achieved some dry nights at 5 years, although nearly 16% would still be described as bedwetters.
- Intensive treatment programmes based on behavioural interventions have shown children as young as 3 years can successfully achieve nocturnal bladder control (Azrin and Theines 1978).

Delayed maturation may, however, increase a child's vulnerability to enuresis, a concept elaborated by MacKeith *et al.* (1973) and Baller (1975), who suggest delayed maturation may create parental apprehension. This, in turn, may lead to parental reactions such as over protection or anxiety which interrupt the developmental process further, creating a cycle of vulnerability where enuresis is the unwelcome result.

Allaying children's fears over immaturity or a fragile nervous system may be achieved in the following ways:

- Where the child has achieved occasional dry nights, this suggests that the necessary maturation of the physical structures has occurred.
- Many children sleeping in unfamiliar circumstances (such as with relatives or on holiday) will achieve some dry nights. Morgan (1981) argues this is because awareness of 'internal' bladder signals increases along with awareness of other 'external' sounds when asleep.
- Appropriate treatment interventions will enable the child to acquire bladder control.

4

Psychological beliefs

*If one is to have an adequate psychology of man, it must
be a psychology of the actor, not the observer.* George
Kelly (1955)

Children invariably hold psychological notions as to why they
continue to wet the bed. They are unfortunately only rarely
asked their opinion. However, a fairly straightforward rating
scale, as illustrated in Fig. 4.1, enables children to discriminate
amongst explanations with relative ease. Individual responses
on such a scale can be followed up and lead to the consideration
of particular treatment interventions. The ten questions may be
categorized with respect to current theoretical ideas about the
aetiology of enuresis which are represented in Fig. 4.2. The
degree of agreement for 50 enuretic children for each psychological notion is also provided with the percentage of children
who construed the notion to be within their control and the
percentage of children who considered the cause to be unstable
or changeable.

Social conditions

Poor living conditions are rarely perceived by children as
causative of bedwettings yet there is reasonably consistent
evidence which suggests children who live in poorer social
environments are more susceptible to enuresis. Such environment include:

- low socio-economic groups (Miller, 1973, Essen and
  Peckham, 1976; Devlin, 1991)
- large, overcrowded families (Miller, 1973; Foxman *et al.*,
  1986)

BELIEFS ABOUT BEDWETTING – PSYCHOLOGICAL

The reason I wet the bed is because:

		Not at all				Very much so		
1.	Poor conditions (cold, damp)	0	1	2	3	4	5	6
2.	Lost the control	0	1	2	3	4	5	6
3.	Fail to wake to full bladder signals	0	1	2	3	4	5	6
4.	Not learnt to hold through the night	0	1	2	3	4	5	6
5.	I get worried and upset	0	1	2	3	4	5	6
6.	I'm afraid to leave my bed to use the toilet	0	1	2	3	4	5	6
7.	It's too much effort	0	1	2	3	4	5	6
8.	I can't be bothered to use the toilet when I wake	0	1	2	3	4	5	6
9.	I go to bed too late	0	1	2	3	4	5	6
10.	I drink too much before bed	0	1	2	3	4	5	6

Figure 4.1. A rating scale to determine the child's beliefs regarding psychological aetiology.

- living in institutional settings (Essen and Peckham, 1976, Stein and Susser, 1967a; 1967b)

Quite what it is about such settings which increase a child's vulnerability to wetting remains unclear. It has been proposed that such conditions increase stress levels which disrupt the acquisition of bladder control (see next section), or that such circumstances provoke parental attitudes such as intolerance which might, in turn, hinder the child's chances of acquiring control. Alternatively, poor social conditions may prevent the production and release of arginine vasopressin, thus causing excessive nocturnal urine production. This formulation is consistent with other socio-biological trigger mechanisms, such as the failure of growth hormones release with children from poor social circumstances (Holland *et al.*, in preparation, Powell *et al.*, 1967)

Key: **Q** = question number from the scale (Figure 4.1)
Mean = level of agreement from n = 50 children
Controllability = % number of children attributing the cause to be within their control
Instability = % number of children attributing the cause to be changeable from day to day

SOCIAL CONDITIONS

Q1

Mean 1.34
Controllability 0%
Instability 60%

INTERRUPTED LEARNING

Q2

Mean 1.22
Controllability 11%
Instability 32%

EMOTIONAL

Q5,6

Mean 2.52
Controllability 41%
Instability 47%

INCOMPLETE LEARNING

Q3,4

Mean 3.94
Controllability 7%
Instability 58%

ATTITUDE

Q7,8

Mean 1.76
Controllability 79%
Instability 71%

BEHAVIOURAL

Q9,10

Mean 1.92
Controllability 69%
Instability 75%

Figure 4.2. Theoretical notions of a psychological nature about the aetiology of nocturnal enuresis.

Interrupted learning

Enuresis, it has been argued, is a consequence of disruptive and stressful events interfering with the acquisition of bladder control. This concept requires some elaboration to account for both primary and secondary enuresis, principally around the issue of vulnerability. With primary enuresis the notion of a 'sensitive period of acquisition' has been proposed, whilst with secondary or onset enuresis, the vulnerability has been discussed in terms of developmental immaturity of the physiological mechanisms. The critical aspects of this theory are as follows:

- The occurrence of a *sensitive stage of acquisition*: MacKeith *et al.* (1973) suggest a sensitive period is typified by a high rate of emergence of the behaviour during the period, and a lower rate of emergence in the periods preceding and following it. Prevalence and longitudinal studies of nocturnal enuresis suggest such a period between 1 and 4 years of age, preceded by a 7–8% emergence in the first year and succeeded by a period where the chances of nocturnal bladder control emerging are about 15% per year (Fergusson *et al.*, 1986; Oppel *et al.*, 1968b).
- The *extended maturational lag* (in cases of secondary enuresis): Jarvelin (1989) found children with nocturnal enuresis at 7 years of age continued to exhibit 'soft signs' of neurological immaturity such as delayed fine and gross motor coordination with perceptual difficulties, supporting the work of Fergusson *et al.* (1986) who discovered delayed measures of motor development was related to the age of attainment of bladder control.
- That stressful or disruptive events *pre-date the enuresis*: there is mounting evidence of a single life event and its ramifications being identified as responsible. Splitting of the family, through separation or divorce is the single most important event pre-dating enuresis (Douglas, 1973; Tissier, 1983; Jarvelin *et al.*, 1990; Jarvelin *et al.*, 1991), with children up to three times more vulnerable to enuresis than children not exposed to such parental separation. Associated with separation comes other potentially adverse stresses including poorer living conditions, emotional turmoil, separation

from siblings and adaptation to new family structures and step-parents. Jarvelin *et al.* (1990) discovered the vulnerable period for the emergence of primary enuresis was around 2–3 years, which probably marks the beginning of toilet training, with stress around this time interfering with the learning or acquisition of bladder control. Both Jarvelin *et al.* (1990) and Fergusson *et al.* (1990) have found an increase in stressful events prior to the occurrence of secondary or onset enuresis.

- The *experience of stress*. Rather than assuming events themselves are stressful, an alternative view considers it is the child's construing and experience of the event which determines its stressfulness (Butler, 1987). Sometimes just the anticipation or threat of an event occurring will be experienced by the child as stressful as the event itself.

There is amongst scholars of child development a belief that a child's separation from mother is a particularly distressing event. Occurring between the first and fourth year, a child's typical reaction to such separation is vigorous protest followed by eventual despair if the separation continues (Bowlby, 1971). However, not all children exposed to the trauma of separation develop enuresis. Douglas (1973) discovered over 50% of children separated from their parents and cared for in unfamiliar surroundings were *not* enuretic.

The interrupted learning hypothesis appears to necessitate three eventualities:

1. A *vulnerability*, either genetically or maturationally determined (as argued by Fergusson *et al.*, 1986 and Jarvelin *et al.*, 1988).
2. The *experience* of distress during a sensitive stage of bladder control acquisition (between 1 and 4 years). Separation from parents, the circumstances accompanying separation and other 'life events' such as moving house or the birth of a sibling (Douglas, 1973) are open to interpretation by the child as stressful. As Green (1986) eloquently suggests: 'no matter how cruel the fate that befalls us, we retain a crucial role in the construction of our own experience'. Thus the way a child makes sense of the event hallmarks the experience as stressful or not.

3. *A mechanism of action*, which assumes anxiety resulting from distress either *interferes* with the process of learning bladder control (see next section), or exerts an effect on bladder functioning through *interference* with the acquisition of normal coordinated muscular responses, leading to unstable detrusor activity (Werry, 1967a; Houts, 1991).

Incomplete learning

Three possibilities suggest themselves:

1. Peterson (1971) argues that bladder control is achieved through aversive conditioning, because pelvis floor relaxation with urination and tactile sensations of urine on the body is normally perceived as aversive. Therefore, contraction of pelvic floor muscles and thus inhibition of urination leads to the *avoidance* of aversive consequences and dryness. However, there may be situations where bedwetting also avoids the aversive consequences:
   i. Where the tactile sensations of urine are *not* perceived as aversive – some children may experience the immediate consequences as warmth. Other children, notably boys, have less skin sensitivity than girls and may not therefore experience the tactile sensations as aversive.
   ii. Where bedwetting is not experienced as aversively as the alternatives, such as waking and toileting in unsatisfactory situations such as cold and damp rooms, an outside toilet, or a toilet difficult to reach (as in attic bedrooms).
2. Bedwetting may be *positively reinforced*, where wetting episodes are immediately followed by positive events. Such events might include the comfort and security offered by parents in consoling a child or encouraging the child to complete the nights' sleep in the parents' own bed.
3. A child is prevented from developing awareness of normal full bladder sensations. Such possibilities arise where parents regulate the frequency of urination through *lifting* or waking to toilet. Christmanson and Lisper (1982) ask the pertinent question of whether parents are governed by the

child's need to toilet, or their own need to *'teach'* the child to be dry, avoid wet beds and the consequent laundry, and escape the pressure from others to have the child dry by a certain age. Lifting, as will be discussed later, tends to lead to the continuation of wetting.

Encouraging parents to become aware of such dynamics is important. It can be difficult to persuade mothers and fathers to alter their behaviour when they believe they are acting in the best interest of the child. However, an invitation to experiment ('let's try and see what happens') will often encourage a change. What parents can be invited to try are:

i.   letting them take more of a back seat, rather than instruct-
     ing, prompting and urging;
ii. allowing the child the opportunity to respond to their own
     internal urges when physiologically ready, by stopping
     lifting;
iii. encouraging parents to be sensitive to the child's increasing
     sense of mastery. Children, given the opportunity, will
     often *choose* the time to try to be dry – they will indicate a
     wish not to wear a nappy for example – and this should
     prompt the parent to respond appropriately.

Behavioural/attitudinal causes

The distinction between behavioural and emotional reactions (next section) is somewhat ill defined for two reasons:

i.   Scales employed to measure the two aspects also fail to
     make the distinction. The Rutter Scale, for example, in-
     cludes both behavioural and emotional items yet amalga-
     mates them to provide an overall score of 'deviance'.
ii. Behaviours may be manifestations of emotional distress.
     Thus thumb sucking (a behaviour) may be the child's way
     of dealing with anxiety, whilst temper tantrums (another
     behaviour) may arise as a consequence of frustration.

Exposition of the link between bedwetting and behaviour has been caught in something of a trap because the search for *associations* between the two, subsequently leads to debate about the nature of the link (if it exists).

Accumulating evidence lends weight to the notion that there is little, if any, evidence of an association between behavioural problems and bedwetting. Parents, when asked to assess their child's behaviour on checklists, tend to place them within a normal range (Couchells *et al.*, 1981; Wagner *et al.*, 1982; Wagner and Matthews, 1985; Wagner and Geffken, 1986). Whilst some individuals do show behavioural problems, as a group, children with enuresis do not display more behavioural problems than other children.

The question remains as to whether there are any behaviours adopted by children which make the acquisition of bladder control more difficult. Figure 4.2 indicates a minority of children do believe their actions contribute to their bedwetting, either in the form of an attitude (lack of effort; not being bothered to use the toilet on waking) or a bedtime behaviour (going to bed too late; drinking too much before bed). Whether such attitudes and actions emerge as a consequence of the bedwetting or are fundamental aetiological factors remains open to debate. However, children who indicate such behaviour as causative number only a few.

Troublesome behaviour may be considered as that which is perplexing to an observer (such as an adult), but which makes perfect sense to the child. Thus parents may be at a loss to understand the child's attitude and behaviour, yet for the child the lack of effort, late bedtime and excessive drinking will be completely meaningful. A child, for example, may choose the immediate gratification of a warm bed on waking with a full bladder, rather than leave the bed to use the toilet.

As Fig. 4.2 indicates, children who volunteer behavioural and attitudinal causes for their bedwetting, feel they are controllable yet unstable. This contrasts sharply with 'biological', emotional and learning formulations, where children attribute the cause as beyond their control.

A minority of mothers also believe their child's bedwetting has behavioural causes – laziness, going to bed too late, and getting back at the parents (Butler *et al.*, 1986; Wagner and Johnson, 1988), and consistent with children's perceptions, attribute these to causes the child has control over. As discussed later, such maternal beliefs lead to annoyance, anger, intolerance and the likelihood of punitive actions (Butler, 1993a; Butler *et al.*, 1994).

Where children ascribe to behavioural or attitudinal causes the therapeutic options include:

- Involving children in experiments where the effect of changing behaviour can be assessed. Thus what difference does it make to the child and his/her relationship with parents if a different behaviour is adopted;
- Understanding the child's choice for acting as he/she does. Thus late bedtimes might arise because the child does not want to miss a favourite TV programme. Would there be alternatives the child can make in such situations?
- With younger children, some strategies of reinforcing more appropriate behaviour might be explored (see section on rewards);
- Tackling intolerant attitude shown by parents (see chapter on families).

Emotional aspects

It seems axiomatic to suggest children with bedwetting experience distress. There are vivid personal accounts by adults who suffered as children (McClean, 1993), late teenagers (Anon, 1987) and children (Butler, 1987) of the humiliation, threat and social alienation experienced because of bedwetting. Some of the evocative descriptions are illustrated in Fig. 1.1 (Chapter 1). Schaefer (1979) believes a common reaction or means of coping with the experience is to present an 'outward indifference' – a stance designed to indicate that it is really of no concern.

Interestingly when adults are asked to comment on bedwetting children they tend to view them as sensitive and tending to shy away from social engagement:

e.g. 'immature' – parents (Couchells *et al.*, 1981);
'sensitive, withdrawn' – social workers (Oppel *et al.*, 1968b);
'submissive, less domineering' – psychologists (Stein and Susser, 1966);

'easy going, easily hurt' – psychiatrists (Kolvin *et al.*, 1972).

Although presenting similar themes, such judgements and appraisals do not indicate that bedwetting children are emotionally maladjusted or distressed. Assessment from parents and others do not fall outside the normal range of emotional adjustment according to Baker (1969), Wagner *et al.* (1982) and Wagner and Matthews (1985). On self report scales, children present a similar story, perceiving themselves in very similar ways to children without enuresis (Baker, 1969; Wagner and Geffken, 1986)

In a recent study children with enuresis were matched by sex and age with children without enuresis, and both were asked to rate themselves on 20 familiar self descriptions, many of them of an emotional nature (e.g. angry, moody, bad tempered). Individual scores, profiles and their implications are discussed in Chapter 6. However, the study indicated that:

- Children with enuresis see themselves as friendly, happy and hardworking.
- Their profiles are not very different on average from non-enuretic children, except children with enuresis tend to perceive themselves as being more frightened, feel different from others, and worry. Fig. 4.3 compares the results of both sets of children.

As Fig. 4.2 illustrates, many children believe emotional factors cause bedwetting, yet this cause is generally outside their control. Interestingly, this confers with mothers' beliefs, as the work of Butler *et al.* (1986) showed worry, being easily upset and lacking in confidence formed the foundation of many mothers understanding of the aetiology. The perception of a lack of control on both mother and child's part suggests there is also a shared sense of helplessness to do anything about the problem.

Psychodynamic models have sought to explain enuresis as a symptom of underlying emotional disturbance, variously hypothesised to be repressed sexuality, anxiety, hostility or dependence. Thus enuresis has been postulated to be:

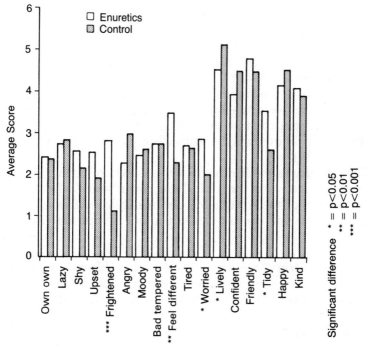

Figure 4.3. Comparison of self descriptions for children with nocturnal enuresis and controls.

- a *displayed* activity where aggression towards parents cannot be expressed directly (Fenichel, 1945);
- a *regressive* symptom which maintains a secure dependent relationship of infancy (Winnicott, 1953);
- a *symbolic* demand for love characterized by weeping through the bladder (Imhof, 1956).

Evidence in support of psychodynamic formulations are difficult to find and all testable hypotheses prove the model to be ill founded:

- Psychotherapeutic approaches focused on assumed underlying disturbances have proved remarkably ineffective in reducing bedwetting (Werry and Cohrssen, 1965; DeLeon and Mandell 1966).

- Children's self reports, ratings and assessment of self, as already discussed, indicate minimal differences of emotional adjustment compared with non-enuretic children, and the differences which do emerge (e.g. feeling different) are perceived to be as a result of enuresis, not the cause.
- Symptomatic treatment (interventions relieving the symptom – the bedwetting – but not the underlying disturbance) such as alarm treatments have proved to be remarkably effective in relieving bedwetting (Doleys, 1977; Forsythe and Butler, 1989).
- The symptom substitution hypothesis (where further symptoms emerge when the underlying disturbance is left unresolved) has proved untenable, because children treated with enuresis alarms do not develop other symptoms (Baker, 1969).

On the contrary, successfully treated children have been shown to improve on measures of self esteem and emotional adjustment (Netley et al., 1984; Moffatt et al., 1987; Moffatt, 1989, 1993).

Interestingly Stromgren and Thomsen (1990) found adults who were enuretic as children felt 'less socialized and more suspicious' than other adults, but on most aspects of psychological functioning there were no differences between the groups.

Whilst the majority of bedwetting children present with no problems of emotional adjustment, there are some children who appear more vulnerable emotionally and in their perception of self. Such children include:

- girls (Rutter et al., 1973);
- children with additional daytime wetting (Rutter et al., 1973; Wagner et al., 1988). Fielding (1980) found day and night wetting children tending to be girls, and it is thus probably the public nature of daytime wetting which may go some way towards explaining their increased vulnerability;
- children who begin wetting after a period of being dry (Rutter et al., 1973; Shaffer, 1980).

The distress, turmoil and upheaval such children experience because of bedwetting, plus the social humiliation from perhaps intolerant parents, uninformed teachers, mischievous siblings and tormenting peers, may according to Werry (1967b), have produced a 'gigantic mythology' whereby all children with enuresis are considered to be emotionally disturbed or troubled. For the small minority that are, support and counselling may prove invaluable in strengthening self belief and resolve, prior to embarking upon a treatment programme to reduce the bedwetting.

For the vast majority of bedwetting children their distress is to be expected. They too will require support and understanding which will be discussed in Chapter 6. However, their emotional reactions are not the expression of any underlying disturbance.

5

Families

*Parents are sometimes a bit of a disappointment to their
children. They don't fulfil the promise of their early
years.* Anthony Powell

Undeniably the family is a complex entity. The diversity of
structure meshed with changing and developing relationships
between its members, gives rise to unique and intricate family
systems. The question, is, what aspects of family life seem to
make it more difficult for a child to accomplish bladder control.
A corollary seeks to understand parental reactions to the
bedwetting and the implications such attitudes and behaviour
have for treatment interventions.

Within this framework, the following points are addressed:

- family structure;
- family relationships;
- parental concerns;
- parental beliefs;
- parental tolerance;
- parental efforts to overcome bedwetting.

Family structure

An appropriate starting point is the composition of a genogram, where parents are asked to record members of the family
who regularly bedwet beyond the age of 5 years. Figure 5.1
provides an example of how a genogram might be compiled.
This will provide information on:

The family unit – which may vary between a nuclear family
(mother and father), through step-families, cohabiting parents

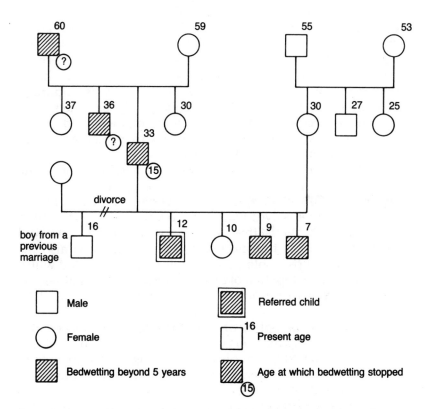

Figure 5.1. Genogram, showing family structure with three generations.

and foster parents to single parent families.

The size of the family – a child from a large family (in terms of number of people living in the house) has an increased risk of nocturnal enuresis (Rutter *et al.*, 1973; Essen and Peckham, 1976; Foxman *et al.*, 1986), as has a child living in overcrowded conditions, defined as the ratio of people to rooms (Tissier, 1983). The rate of enuresis may not be a function of large and overcrowded conditions as such, but as discussed in Chapter 4, a result of living in poorer socio-economic conditions which may through the suppression of AVP give rise to nocturnal polyuria and enuresis (Holland *et al.*, in preparation)

Birth order – the relationship between birth order and noctur- nal enuresis has produced equivocal findings. It has been vari- ously proposed that the first born (Meadow, 1980), the middle child (Devlin, 1991) or the fourth or later child (Essen and Peckham, 1976) are more prone to nocturnal enuresis. Perhaps it is not the birth rank itself which is important, but the child's perception of his role within the family which is important (Butler, 1987). Thus a first-born child might be reluctant to become dry because it may threaten the mother–child attach- ment, whereas a later born child may wish to preserve a depen- dent and special bond with mother.

Family history of enuresis – the issue of a possible genetic link was discussed in Chapter 3. There is a strong probability, in the region of a 70% chance, that a bedwetting child will have a parent who themselves was also a bedwetter (Bakwin, 1971; Fielding, 1980). Whilst this suggests a vulnerability to delayed bladder control is transmitted genetically, there is also the possibility that psychological variables are transmitted which impede the development of bladder control. For example, par- ents who were bedwetters themselves may:

i.   be more accepting of bedwetting in their children. It is interesting that Fergusson *et al.* (1986) discovered that delayed toilet training, which might be a marker of parental acceptance, was related to slower attainment of bladder control;

ii. hold beliefs about bedwetting which leave them with a sense of helplessness (Butler *et al.*, 1986). Thus a belief that deep sleep is causative might discourage parents from providing a climate conducive to the development of bladder control;

iii. adopt inappropriate measures to which they them- selves were subject as children. Miller (1973) postulates that parenthood is often the repetition of a theme, a theme experienced at first as a child. Thus measures such as lifting, fluid restriction or punishment, which can reduce the development of bladder control, may be adopted more stringently than parents who were not former enuretics;

iv. live in more stressful circumstances (Devlin, 1991), par- ticularly of a socio-economic nature, so that the emotional and financial burden of coping with wet beds creates a tense and punitive environment not conducive to the development of bladder control.

Family relationships

Following analysis of the family structure, the relationships between family members can prove important. Relevant to nocturnal enuresis, the following indicators should be considered:

Financial hardship – bedwetting is a costly problem with the extra laundry, mattress covering, replacement bedding and wear and tear of washing machines (Dobson, 1993; Norgaard, 1993). A number of studies have also shown that bedwetting is more prevalent in families where the father is unemployed or works manually (Couchells *et al.*, 1981; Tissier, 1983; Devlin, 1991; Jarvelin *et al.*, 1991).

Maternal stress – mothers of enuresis children tend to be younger than mothers of non-enuretic children (Douglas, 1973; Nilsson *et al.*, 1973). Whether this suggests less skilled parenting or increased stress levels with greater intolerance of bedwetting (Morgan and Young, 1975) remains open to question.

Separation from mother – loss or separation from mother during a child's early years occurs more in the history of bedwetting children than those who develop bladder control (Douglas; 1973; Shaffer, 1973).

Disruption – families characterised by parental disharmony and discord are more likely to have children who wet the bed (Douglas, 1973; Tissier, 1983), and be less likely to respond effectively to treatment. Dische *et al.* (1983) define various aspect of family disruption:

- serious marital discord;
- parental mental illness;
- presence of a physically or mentally handicapped child.

Johnson (1980) has pointed out that nocturnal enuresis is not inevitably the result of stress or disturbance within the family, as many children with an emotionally stable and secure relationship with their parents can develop nocturnal enuresis, and on the other hand, children from severely disrupted families will develop bladder control. It is perhaps not the event itself which is stressful, but the parental and child's interpretation of the event which marks it as stressful.

Coalitions – families can be distinguished by the patterns of alliances between the members (Frude, 1991). A type of family process often seen in families with an enuretic child, according to Protinsky and Dillard (1983), is the *stable coalition*. This is where one parent is over involved or enmeshed with the enuretic child, whilst the other parent is relatively peripheral or disengaged. Here therapeutic involvement might involve a restructuring of the relationships whereby the peripheral parent is put in charge of helping the enuretic child through taking on the chores of washing and the recording of progress. Butler *et al.* (1986) also advocated sharing the burden of extra laundry amongst family members in order to relieve mothers who otherwise may become intolerant and angry towards the child.

Parental concerns

Most work in the following three sections has been directed at understanding the mother's perspective rather than fathers, although an investigation by Woolnough (1991) suggested a similarity between parents in the way they understood and reacted to their child's enuresis. Foxman *et al.* (1986) found parents tended to worry more about girls that boys. Table 5.1 illustrates aspects of bedwetting that mothers find most troubling.

Table 5.1. Maternal concerns over bedwetting.

	Mean agreement (0–6 Scale)
Emotional impact	4.48
Effect on social relationships	4.02
Normality – should have outgrown it by now	3.93
Removing the smell from the bedroom	3.84
Keeping it a secret	3.48
The extra washing	3.18
Financial repercussions	1.70
That parent might be to blame	1.32

Mothers' principal concerns are for the emotional and social well-being of their children which is particularly noticeable where bedwetting is construed as having an emotional source such as anxiety or loss of confidence (Butler *et al.*, 1986). The concerns are very real. In Chapter 1 the emotional sequelae of bedwetting were discussed, and might include shame, acute embarrassment and a dread of discovery. Whilst most studies suggest bedwetting children are emotionally well adjusted (Couchells *et al.*, 1981; Butler *et al.*, 1994) there is also compelling evidence to suggest that when children do learn to acquire nocturnal bladder control they experience a sense of accomplishment and increase in self esteem (Netley *et al.*, 1984; Moffatt *et al.*, 1987; Moffatt, 1989).

The fear of discovery and upset experienced by the child may lead to withdrawal from others, especially on social occasions. Thus maternal concern over problematic social relationships is also valid. The upshot of being a bedwetter may indeed lead to a restricted social life. A survey of events which bedwetting children were felt to be prevented from participating in, according to mothers includes:

Staying at friends overnight 73%
School trips with a sleep over 63%
Staying with relatives overnight 45%
Joining clubs (e.g. Scouts, Guides) 36%

(Butler, 1987)

Of less concern for most mothers are the issues of coping with the problem – removing the smell, and extra laundry – and keeping it a well guarded secret. It is, however, important to identify individual mothers who show more concern over the smell and extra washing than concern over their child's emotional and social welfare, because such mothers are likely to develop intolerant attitudes towards the child (Butler *et al.*, 1986) that require particular interventions which will be discussed later. Although the financial repercussions were considered quite low on the list of maternal concerns, the cost of washing and drying bedding, replacing pyjamas and sheets, and purchasing bedding protection for a child who wets three times a week can amount to approximately £9.00 per week (Dobson, 1993).

Beliefs over cause

Many biological and psychological theories have been proposed to explain the aetiology of nocturnal enuresis. By far the most heavily endorsed maternal view is that of deep sleep (Klackenberg, 1981; Butler *et al.*, 1986), an opinion entirely in concordance with children's beliefs, and yet as discussed in Chapter 3, a view inconsistent with research findings on sleep and enuresis. Other notions about aetiology commonly expressed by mothers include emotional reasons (e.g. the child's sensitivity, susceptibility to emotional upset) and a belief that vulnerability to enuresis is passed on genetically.

The common ground these three beliefs (deep sleep, emotional cause and genetic predisposition) share is that they are considered to be *internal* (something to do with the child), *stable* (do not change from day to day) and *uncontrollable* (nothing the child can do about it). Attributional theory (Antaki and Brewin, 1982) suggests such perceptions lead to a feeling of *helplessness* – an inability to do anything to assist in a meaningful way. This model is outlined in Fig. 5.2 and is well supported by research

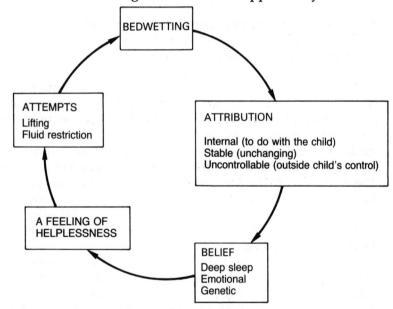

Figure 5.2. A model descriptive of the way most mothers understand and cope with bedwetting.

findings (Butler *et al.*, 1986, 1993). Mothers resort, often in desperation, to 'logical' options such as lifting and fluid restriction, which as discussed later, may only serve to maintain the enuresis. Perhaps the most befitting approach is to enable parents to feel supported and continue being supportive towards their child.

This may involve:

* Practical advice – on bedding protection (Appendix C);
  – on sleeping bag covers (Appendix C);
  – on removing the smell (Appendix C).
* Education – exploring the deep sleep myth;
  – reassurance concerning the child's emotional adjustment;
  – developing beliefs about the lack of bladder signal recognition.
* reassurance – the common feeling of helplessness;
  – the need for their continued involvement with patience, support and encouragement.
* assessing expectations – the rate of spontaneous recovery;
  – the rates of improvement expected with different treatment options.
* improve understanding – enabling parents to see what their child considers important about the enuresis.
* develop treatment strategies involving the enuresis alarm.

Whilst most mothers consider bedwetting to be outside the child's control, and consequently feel helpless to do anything about the problem, a small proportion of mothers perceive that the enuresis is controllable by the child (Butler *et al.*, 1986). Such mothers tend to feel annoyed and angry about the bedwetting and present an altogether different picture, from mothers who construe their child's bedwetting as uncontrollable. This will be the focus of the next section.

Parental tolerance

Morgan and Young (1975) developed a 20-item scale for measuring maternal tolerance/intolerance of nocturnal enuresis. It has proved to be a particularly sensitive instrument in detecting maternal feelings. Recently the scale has been cross-vali-

Please circle YES if the following statement describes how you feel, or circle NO if the statement does not describe how you feel

1. I feel sorry for any child who wets the bed	YES	NO
2. I try to help him/her not to be upset	YES	NO
3. It's a pity the bedwetting stops him/her doing so many things	YES	NO
4. It's embarrassing to be a bedwetter	YES	NO
5. I don't mind the washing because he/she can't help it	YES	NO
6. I tell him/her it does not matter	YES	NO
7. Bedwetting usually clears up on its own	YES	NO
8. I find it difficult to get used to the wet beds	YES	NO
9. After a wet bed I show him/her I am disappointed	YES	NO
10. I try to make him/her realize the unpleasantness the bedwetting causes for others	YES	NO
11. The bedwetting is a nuisance to the rest of us	YES	NO
12. I don't see why my child can't be dry when other children can	YES	NO
13. Children could stop bedwetting if they tried hard enough	YES	NO
14. If he/she would grow up a bit we wouldn't have all the trouble with wet beds	YES	NO
15. I punish my child for bedwetting	YES	NO
16. A smack following bedwetting never did any harm	YES	NO

Figure 5.3. Feelings about bedwetting.

dated and adapted to improve administration and scoring (Butler *et al.*, 1993). The adapted scale is illustrated in Fig. 5.3. It consists of 16 items, to which parents are asked to respond affirmatively or negatively. Items progressively measure increasingly intolerant attitudes, so affirmative response to items numbered 8–16 suggest intolerance. The degree of intolerance can be estimated by adding up the number of YES responses on items 8–16; the higher the number, the more intolerant the feeling.

Intolerant maternal attitudes have been found to be associated with:

- anger and annoyance over bed wetting (Butler *et al.*, 1986);
- older children (Butler *et al.*, 1986);

- families from less skilled socio-economic backgrounds (Morgan and Young, 1975), where coping with enuresis in less adequate housing and overcrowded conditions might be considered particularly disheartening;
- increased concern over the consequence of bedwetting such as the burden of extra washing and the residual smell (Butler *et al.*, 1986);
- a perception of enuresis as *controllable* by the child, leading mothers to consider negative aspect of the child's behaviour, such as laziness, to be contributing to the problem. This subsequently results in the mother taking a more critical and rejecting stance towards the child (Butler *et al.*, 1986; Wagner and Johnson, 1988);
- the development of increasingly more punitive measures being taken towards the child (Butler *et al.*, 1993). Figure 5.4 illustrates a representation of the development of intolerance. It is of concern that about a third of mothers admit to taking punitive actions contingent upon bedwetting (White, 1971; Butler, 1987), and non-accidental injury has been reported to be associated with increased rates of bedwetting (Tissier, 1983);
- an increased incidence of drop out or early withdrawal from alarm based treatment (Morgan and Young, 1975; Butler *et*

Figures indicate the percentage of mothers taking such actions towards their bedwetting child.

Shows disappointment	43%
Feels it's a nuisance	30%
Try to make child realise the unpleasantness it causes others	27%
Believe the child is not trying hard enough	14%
Believe the bedwetting is a dirty habit	2%
Resort to smacking	1.5%

Figure 5.4. A representation of developing maternal intolerance (from Butler, Redfern and Forsythe, 1993).

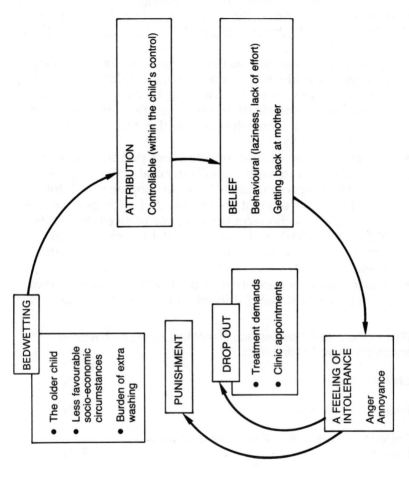

Figure 5.5. A model of the spiral of maternal intolerance.

al., 1988; Wagner *et al.*, 1982), which may be related to intolerance towards the demands of conditioning treatment (Wagner *et al.*, 1982), or of attending clinic appointments (Morgan and Young, 1975).

The model of developing maternal intolerance is illustrated in Fig. 5.5. Without doubt the course of action with such intolerant mothers must be aimed at securing their continued attendance at appointments. Not to do so increases the risk of increased intolerance, escalating and prolonged punitive reactions and the possible threat of physical abuse towards the child. A survey of over 5000 children in the USA (Strauss and Gelles, 1986) found the following annual incidence of punitive and violent parental acts towards children aged 3–17 years:

i. Slapping, spanking, pushing, grabbing – 63%;
ii. kicking, biting, hitting with a fist, beating up, threats with a knife or gun – 36%.

The author regarded only those in category (ii) as physical abuse. Almost all the variables found to be associated with an intolerant attitude towards enuresis, have similarly been related to physical abuse of children:

• Parents of a lower socio-economic background with poverty, poor housing, unemployment and lower educational history are at a higher risk of abusing their children (Frude, 1991).
• Where parents develop a critical attitude with a tendency to blame the child, plus a lack of effective ways of managing the child's behaviour, the risk of physical abuse is increased (Frude, 1991).
• Abusive mothers often attribute a child's annoying behaviour to internal controllable factors such as personality or defiance, and are likely to attribute negative characteristics to their children even when there is no valid reason for such judgements (Richman *et al.*, 1982; Larrence and Twentyman, 1983).
• Children vulnerable to physical abuse are likely to be those who make extra demands on parental time, effort and money, which when parents are poor or have few resources,

may prove especially costly and irritating, increasing the stress and demands on parents (Belsky and Vondra, 1987).
- A relatively high number of older abused children are enuretic (Frude, 1991).

The protracted nature of alarm treatment for children with enuresis proves too demanding for intolerant parents who tend to drop out of treatment and may feel increasingly resentful and angry towards the child. The presence of maternal intolerance at a first appointment should therefore indicate:

- The prescription of medication (preferably desmopressin) to immediately improve the child's chances of dry nights, reduce maternal desperation and annoyance and begin to establish a sense of confidence with the child. The problems of relapse with the removal of desmopressin are well documented, yet programmes have now been developed to prevent much of this. These will be discussed in Chapter 12.
- The need to encourage other members of the family to help the child cope with the enuresis, so that the laundry, for example, might be shared between parents and siblings encouraged to support the child.
- The necessity of supporting mothers through regular contact, the development of non-critical attitudes (e.g. that enuresis is *not* controllable), and improving their ability to manage the child's behaviour without resorting to punitive actions.

Parental efforts to overcome bedwetting

Table 5.2 presents the measures parents most usually adopt in order to help children overcome bedwetting.

Lifting

In all three surveys of parental efforts, lifting or raising the child during the night to toilet has been the most common practice employed. During a child's early years lifting is often undertaken as a way of achieving two objectives: to help the child achieve a dry bed and, as Baller (1975) suggests, to do this without waking the child, so averting any fuss created by the

Table 5.2. Frequency of measures (%), adopted by parents from three surveys.

Measure		Butler (1987)	Novello and Novello (1987)	Wagner and Johnson (1988)
	Country	UK	USA	USA
	n=	100	346	47
Lifting		97	84	89
Restricting fluids		88	68	83
Medication		74	14	34
Rewards		54	53	51
Have child change the wet bed		40	–	–
Punishment		37	36	9
Talk about the problem		–	80	–

child being disturbed. Paradoxically, the more successful parents are in achieving these two objectives, the more likely the child is to continue bedwetting. The problems associated with lifting are many fold:

- If the child is not woken when toileted, the child is, in effect, encouraged to empty the bladder whilst asleep, thus engineering the opposite response to that which is intended. Baller (1975) suggests lifting 'teaches the child to urinate whilst asleep'.
- The bladder may be trained to empty at certain times, particularly if parents lift at a regular time such as their own bedtime (Morgan and Young, 1972a, 1972b).
- The bladder is unlikely to be full at the time of lifting, and therefore the association between a full bladder and waking is not given the opportunity to develop. As Morgan (1981) indicates this does not enable, and in many ways denies, the child the opportunity to develop bladder control.
- Any subsequent dry beds may encourage parents to continue lifting, and thus create the child's dependence on them to regulate toileting. It is enlightening to discover that Christmanson and Lisper (1982) found parents who continued lifting children in the early years tended to have children who were more likely to wet the bed than parents whose children were not lifted.

The clear message seems to be a recommendation to *stop* lifting as soon as possible. The possibility of employing waking strategies (random or structured) are discussed in Chapter 10.

Restricting fluids

The second most commonly reported venture employed by mothers, restricting fluid, usually means discouraging drinks at supper time. However, with some families the restriction may be enforced from when the child comes home from school. The assumption upon which this action is taken is that the bladder will not have to hold as much urine throughout the night and therefore the point at which urination is triggered will not be reached. The consensus of opinion suggests that fluid restriction is not helpful and may, on the contrary, lead to prolonged bedwetting. Morgan (1981) takes this view and argues that fluid restriction tends to cause the bladder to adjust to coping with lower volumes of urine, and thus bladder contractions (the signal for urination) occur at less than maximum levels. The child's ability to hold thus becomes impaired with the possibility that the bladder develops a low functional capacity. The commonsense recommendation, which often pleases children, is:

- to encourage a small drink in the last hour before bed;
- to drink non-diuretics at this time (i.e. *not* tea, coffee or fizzy drinks).

Reward systems

Interestingly, Table 5.2 illustrates that in all three surveys approximately 50% of mothers had tried a system of rewards, whether it be star charts, promises of treats or monetary benefits contingent on dry nights. Butler (1987) found that of all measures used by mothers, reward schemes were the most readily given up – with only 7% employing such methods at the time of a clinic appointment. Mothers then clearly perceive reward schemes as ineffective. The problems with reward schemes consist of:

i. The criteria are often set too high and unachievable. Mothers for example might promise a bike if the child 'stops wetting the bed'. This presents the child with an overwhelming task and any behaviour appropriate to achieving a dry night fails to be recognized or rewarded. Thus many children fail to acquire the reward, which both increases that sense of despair and helplessness and discourages parents from adopting a 'positive' approach.

ii. When children do manage to achieve sufficient dry nights to secure a reward, it is rare that parents present the reward immediately or consistently. More usually the child has to wait until the weekend, until the parents have saved up sufficient funds, or as an extra on a birthday. Thus the child's behaviour fails to be reinforced or rewarded at the appropriate moment with the subsequent feeling, for the child, of being let down.

iii. The presentation of a reward for achieving something the child is motivated to do anyway (such as acquiring dry beds), may only serve to *reduce* the intrinsic pleasure in mastering the skill (Harter, 1978)

iv. If rewards are attached to the achievement of dry nights it implies that effort (or lack of it) on the child's behalf is involved. Where rewards are considered useful they need to be applied to behaviours (such as using the toilet before bed, or waking to toilet) which lead to the achievement of a dry night, rather than applied to the dry night itself. In this way appropriate behaviours are rewarded, not the outcome.

v. Rewards may be considered ethically suspect. They imply, for many parents, an act of bribery. However, bribery is usually considered to be an attempt to corrupt or influence people to act immorally. Where rewards are employed to assist children in attaining socially acceptable behaviour, the allegation of bribery seems unfounded.

When reward systems are employed some essential steps are suggested:

• As a reward, negotiate with the child and parent something

THINGS I WOULD LIKE TO DO

1. Hire a video   10 points
2. Go swimming   15 points
3. Go fishing   25 points
4. Go to the cinema   30 points
5. Theme park   50 points

Behaviours	Mon	Tues	Wed	Thur	Fri	Sat	Sun
1. Toilet before bed (1 point)							
2. Wake by self to toilet (2 points)							
3. Wake to the alarm (1 point)							
4. Wake quickly – small patch (1 point)							
5. Dry night (3 points)							
TOTAL POINTS							

Figure 5.6. A reward scheme based on a points system.

he/she wishes to *do* rather than something he/she wants to have. This avoids the escalation into increasingly more costly tangible rewards, such as promises of a mountain bike or computer console. It can also involve the whole family in sharing the activity, so the child is not seen by siblings to be treated unfairly. Figure 5.6 illustrates a structured means of applying such a reward scheme. A number of points are ascribed to each chosen activity by the parent.

* Reward achievable behaviours, and those which are appropriate to enabling the child to accomplish dry nights. As in Fig. 5.6 a certain number of points are made contingent on each behaviour, with the child totalling these up as he/she performs them.
* Rewards should be made available as soon as the total is achieved. The child will have the choice in Fig. 5.6 to exchange the 10 points he collects for the hire of a video, or may choose to save these and work for extra points for a greater reward. In this way the child assumes greater control over his/her behaviour and the reward contingent upon it.

Having the child change the bed

Wagner and Geffken (1986) found children aged 5–7 years reported that their mothers took the responsibility for changing wet sheets, whereas older children were expected to remove and often wash their own bedclothes and sheets. As maternal intolerance increases with age (Butler *et al.*, 1986) it may be that having the child change his own sheets is an expression of maternal intolerance. It is disconcerting that 75% of mothers who insist on the child changing the sheets, continue to apply this despite its ineffectiveness (Butler, 1987). For parents it might serve either as a punishment (an aversive consequence contingent on a wet bed), or as a means of transferring responsibility to the child.

It becomes important to determine the reason for the parent's approach because many treatment programmes advocate the child's involvement in removing wet sheets and re-making the bed, as a way of encouraging greater responsibility. If, however, the procedure has punitive overtones for the child, then he/she may attempt to avoid or sabotage the treatment programme.

6
The child's notions

The only thing that can ever defeat you is yourself
Robert Stroud (The Birdman of Alcatraz)

Children strive to make sense of their bedwetting. They formulate ideas about causality, and the 'why me' syndrome; they conjecture about the frailty of their waterworks; they have inklings about being alone with the problem; and they make educated guesses about what to do to resolve the difficulty.

Composing an understanding of the child's perspective follows from asking questions; questions which Ravenette (1977) suggest should enable the child to feel free to respond whilst also being penetrative for the interviewer. Often an obstacle to understanding is the way our traditional methods of assessment – the standardized questionnaire – seeks to gather 'grains of truth' by asking questions framed in our own terms of reference. By contrast, methods which seek to engage children in conversation, structured by the interviewer and constructed in ways meaningful to children, have a better chance of understanding the child's own understanding. This places us in a better position to discover how a child makes sense of him/herself and the problem.

Interviews need structure. They enable the verbally inhibited to inform and the garrulous to be contained. The invention of perceptive questions may, at the very least, invite responses which lead to decisions about appropriate treatment interventions. Occasionally the bonus is a child who, by grappling with the question, will make the first step towards resolving the problem.

An interview with the child might begin with a statement of our purpose. It might start something like 'I am interested to know how you make sense of things, to learn what bothers you about the bedwetting and how we can begin to work out the best ways of helping.' The questions which follow will then be organized to this end. A format suggested by Butler (1993b) is as follows:

- Beliefs over cause.
- Impact on lifestyle.
- Impact on self.
- Perceived family attitudes.
- Efforts.
- Problematic implications.

Beliefs over cause

Aetiological theories, both biological and psychological, have been reviewed in Chapters 2 and 3. Grasping an idea of the child's perception of bedwetting can be obtained by using the questionnaire shown in Fig. 6.1. This identifies in children's terms, 16 aetiological possibilities regarding the cause of nocturnal enuresis and combines questions from Table 3.1 (biological causes) and, Fig. 4.1 (psychological causes). Children are

BELIEFS ABOUT BEDWETTING

The reason I wet the bed is because:

		Not at all				Very much so		
1.	Deep sleep	0	1	2	3	4	5	6
2.	It runs in the family	0	1	2	3	4	5	6
3.	I make too much urine	0	1	2	3	4	5	6
4.	It's a physical problem	0	1	2	3	4	5	6
5.	It's painful passing urine	0	1	2	3	4	5	6
6.	Can't hold throughout the night	0	1	2	3	4	5	6
7.	My bladder doesn't work properly	0	1	2	3	4	5	6
8.	My bladder has not fully developed yet	0	1	2	3	4	5	6
9.	Poor conditions (e.g. damp, cold)	0	1	2	3	4	5	6
10.	Lost the ability I once had	0	1	2	3	4	5	6
11.	Failure to wake to full bladder signals	0	1	2	3	4	5	6
12.	I get worried and upset	0	1	2	3	4	5	6
13.	It's too much effort	0	1	2	3	4	5	6
14.	I drink too much before bed	0	1	2	3	4	5	6
15.	I'm often in trouble	0	1	2	3	4	5	6
16.	A way of getting back at mum	0	1	2	3	4	5	6

Figure 6.1. Beliefs about bedwetting: Questionnaire over cause.

asked to respond to each item by using a 0–6 rating scale anchored with 'not at all' and 'very much so'. The theories to which each statement relates are contained in Table 3.1 and Fig. 4.2. From 8 years upwards children find the request to employ a rating scale quite within their task. For children who struggle to comprehend, the clearest explanation is to encourage them to see that the more strongly they feel the item describes why they bedwet, the higher score (rating) would be given. It is important to emphasize to children that there are *no* right or wrong answers, but that we are using this scale to help in *understanding* the child's views. The predominant beliefs of children are presented in Table 3.1 and Fig. 4.2.

The implications for children responding highly on some of the items are:

- *Deep sleep*: the most heavily endorsed view, and consistent with that expressed by mothers (Butler *et al.*, 1986), with approximately two-thirds of children rating highly. It is, as with all biological causes, considered to be outside the child's control.

  Deep sleep as a cause of enuresis, as discussed in Chapter 3, has no scientific support. Yet it remains an enduring myth. For the child it is important to suggest a shift from belief in deep sleep to *difficulty of arousing from sleep*. Most children will volunteer occasions when they can, or will, wake from sleep – when ill, the noise of a torrential storm, or a bad dream – suggesting *it is possible* to wake when it is important. This is a powerful concept for the child to take on board, for if he/she acknowledges that signals which are important will wake him/her, then the grounds for using an enuresis alarm, which will signal the need to wake by buzzing, will have been laid. An interesting experiment to set a child is to ask him/her to set an *internal* alarm clock – to tell him/herself to wake next morning at a specified time – and to record the results of this. Success with such a task suggests the child will wake up to the signal of an enuresis alarm or be amenable to wake with self suggestions (Chapter 10).

- *Failure to wake to full bladder signals; can't hold throughout the night; bladder doesn't work properly*: these three are all rated relatively highly and perceived as uncontrollable. They provide the opportunity to reinforce the notion concerning lack of bladder signal awareness. Children might be helped to see that becoming dry will *either* involve:

– learning to wake to toilet when the bladder is full; or
– learning to hold throughout the night.

Thus the build-up to using the enuresis alarm or self suggestions will again have been achieved.

- *Drink too much before bed*: this is considered possible by many children, and construed as within their control. It may lead to fluid restriction, which is commonly imposed by mothers (Butler, 1987), and is the most likely method children adopt themselves to control the bedwetting. The problems of fluid restriction have already been noted, and possibly leads to the development of lowered functional bladder capacity. As Mark Twain offered, 'water taken in moderation cannot hurt anyone', and children should be reassured that a small drink before bed will not be harmful.
- *Make too much urine*: this might lead children to take a similar step, and reduce fluids. It is relevant to stress that the volume of urine made bears little relationship to the chances of becoming dry, because as stated earlier, dryness is achieved through learning to wake or learning to retain throughout the night.
- *Emotional*: the child's anxieties and distress may be a consequence of the bedwetting rather than a cause, and this needs to be acknowledged. Detailed recording will illuminate if stressful events tend to provoke bedwetting, such as beginning school after the weekend, or holiday. A further source can lie in the child's fears of leaving the bed to toilet, which may be rectified by allowing the child a torch, or providing a receptacle in the room for the child to urinate in.
- *Physical problem: bladder not fully developed*: medical screening should exclude any physical abnormality. According to Sorotzkin (1984) an estimate of anatomical abnormality of the bladder or urinary track is no more than 10%, most of whom will also have associated daytime wetting. Although bedwetting children are vulnerable to urinary tract infections, these are not usually the cause of nocturnal enuresis.

Antibiotic medication will clear up the infection but the majority of children will continue to wet the bed. Children value the reassurance that there is nothing physically wrong. They are also relieved to learn that the occurrence of any dry nights indicates their bladder and associated mechanisms are fully developed and mature.

- *Too much effort*: children who acknowledge this as a reason for their bedwetting also tend to perceive it as within their control. A familiar scenario is the child, who wakes to urinate, but turns over and returns to sleep, subsequently having a wetting episode. What acts to prevent the child toileting may be a reluctance to leave a warm bed, or have to fully wake up, or even an inaccessible toilet. Steps such as a reward (small token) in the toilet or a receptacle in the bedroom may go a long way to assisting the child achieve dry nights.
- *Runs in the family*: on the whole this reason is not heavily endorsed. However, there tends to be a bimodal distribution, with children rating 0 or 5 and 6 and rarely rating in the middle of the scale. This occurs because children seem either to know of the presence, or not, of bed wetting within their parents.

The final four views – in trouble (behavioural), lost the ability (usually applying only to secondary enuresis), poor conditions, and getting back at mum (psychoanalytical) are rarely singled out by children as major reasons for bedwetting.

Impact on lifestyle

The issue here is concerned with how the bedwetting pervades the child's life, and to this end the following questions may be posed:

- What are the bad things (disadvantages) about bedwetting?
- What does the bedwetting prevent you from doing?
- What difference would it make to be dry?

Below is the response of a 10-year-old girl to the contrasting questions of the disadvantages of wetting the advantages of becoming dry.

Disadvantages of wetting	*Advantages of becoming dry*
feels uncomfortable	warm, cosy in the morning
quilt gets wet	quilt stays dry
feel sad and upset	feel happy that something might have worked
mum has the extra washing	mum feels it will be great
smelly	room won't smell
can't lie in	can have a sleep in at the weekend
feel different from others	feel just the same as your friends.

Such responses inform and enlighten the child's plight. They exhibit:

- The *broadness* of impact. The consequences of bedwetting for this girl are probably far-reaching. With other children the impact may be far less or sometimes quite specific. For example, one 12-year-old boy construed the problem in terms of time: 'it makes you late, I have to wash and might miss something on telly, if friends call, sometimes I'm not ready because I'm putting my clothes on.' (Butler, 1987).
- The *anticipation* of change. Faced with persistent bed wetting, many children's conception of reality is framed by the problem. They experience the effects so often, it becomes a way of being. Inviting children to seek the contrast – the advantages of being dry – often opens up the possibility for children to consider, to verbalize ideas perhaps not previously formulated. There emerges a different and contrasting perspective, with the possibility that the child will become active and engaged in solving the problem.
- The *decision* to change. Bannister (1986) suggests change, of a psychological nature, involving two processes – the *why* (why become dry), and *how* (how dryness is achieved). Those children who generate notions concerning the advantages of being dry have initiated the first stage and await appropriate interventions to enable dryness to be achieved.

The most commonly expressed effects of bedwetting have been formulated into a questionnaire, presented in Fig. 6.2. It consists of 17 statements to which the child is asked to respond 'no', 'sometimes' or 'yes' as to whether it applies or not. 'Yes'

IMPACT OF BEDWETTING

Name . . . .

How is it for you:

1.	Mum has a lot of extra washing	NO	SOMETIMES	YES
2.	It feels cold when I wake up	NO	SOMETIMES	YES
3.	My bedroom smells	NO	SOMETIMES	YES
4.	I have to have a bath/shower each morning	NO	SOMETIMES	YES
5.	I have to keep friends out of my room	NO	SOMETIMES	YES
6.	Drinks are stopped before bedtime	NO	SOMETIMES	YES
7.	I have to change my own bed	NO	SOMETIMES	YES
8.	I have to go to bed early	NO	SOMETIMES	YES
9.	I have to get up straight away	NO	SOMETIMES	YES
10.	Mum/dad get upset with me	NO	SOMETIMES	YES
11.	Brother/sister tease me	NO	SOMETIMES	YES
12.	I get upset about the bedwetting	NO	SOMETIMES	YES
13.	I'm afraid others might find out	NO	SOMETIMES	YES
14.	I feel different from my friends	NO	SOMETIMES	YES
15.	Sleeping over at my friend's house is impossible	NO	SOMETIMES	YES
16.	Having friends to stay over is difficult	NO	SOMETIMES	YES
17.	School trips to sleep overnight are out	NO	SOMETIMES	YES

Figure 6.2. Questionnaire concerning perceived impact of bedwetting.

responses imply impact and are scored 2; 'sometimes' responses are scored 1; and 'no' responses implying lack of impact, are scored 0. The scale has been factor analysed revealing 8 distinct factors subdivided into psychological and non-psychological concerns (Butler *et al.*, 1994):

- *Psychological*
  1. Lack of socialization – unable to sleep over, go on trips, have friends to sleep.

2. Fear of discovery – fearing others finding out.
3. Sense of difference – feel different from friends.
4. Emotional reaction – sadness, upset.

- *Non-psychological*
  5. Physical consequences – extra washing, cold when wake.
  6. Hygiene – room smells, bath each morning, can't have friends in room to play.
  7. Contingencies – no drink before bed, have to change the bed.
  8. Time in bed – can't stay up, can't lie in.

Some interesting results have emerged from using this scale:

- The most frequently expressed consequences are:
  – fear of others finding out;
  – unable to sleep at friends;
  – feel different from friends.

(Butler *et al.*, 1994)

With the availability of medication, such as desmopressin, bedwetting should no longer be the cause of widespread social withdrawal and fears of isolation and alienation. Invitations to sleep over or attend school trips can be made increasingly more acceptable because of medication and the following advice:

i. The probability of being dry when sleeping somewhere different. This phenomenon is well known and explained by Morgan (1981) as a reflection of the body's increased sense of awareness (both internal and external) when sleeping somewhere unusual.
ii. The availability of bedding protection and sleeping bag covers (see Appendix C).
iii. The ingenuity of childhood. Prior to a camping trip an 11-year-old boy decided to sleep at the edge of the tent so that if he had a wetting episode he could excuse himself by suggesting it was the morning dew.
iv. The gathering understand of many teachers and camp leaders with the accompanying reduction in the stigma attached to bedwetting.

- The increased chance of successful treatment with an alarm when the problem is construed psychologically (Butler *et al.*, 1990a; Butler *et al.*, 1994). The scale (Fig. 6.2) is constructed in a way so that non-psychological items form the initial statements and psychological items the latter statements. This enables the user to quickly determine how the child construes the impact of bedwetting. Where children do not regard their enuresis as having psychological consequences, it makes sense to raise their awareness to such possibilities because, if not at the present, it would seem palpably true that at some time in the future, if the bedwetting persists, the child will be faced with the psychological consequences. Consideration might be given to exploring the solutions: e.g. 'What would it be like to be able to sleep over at your friends?' or 'what would it feel like to wake up each morning dry?'

Impact on self

In general, as discussed in Chapter 4, there seems little to distinguish children with enuresis from those without, on measures of self image and self esteem. This, of course, masks the variety of individual reactions. A technique for unearthing the impact bedwetting has on a child's vision of self is illustrated in Fig. 6.3 with the self image scale. The 20 self descriptions are child generated, thus holding appeal and familiarity for children. In presenting the scale children are invited to score themselves (from 0 to 6) on each item with higher ratings representing a strong belief that the description characterizes themselves. Figure 6.4 shows a profile typical of many children with enuresis (Butler, 1993b). Ratings are high on most of the *'positive'* descriptions (1–7) and low on the *negative* descriptions (9–20). The exceptions are items 9 (feel different) and 18 (frightened). These two descriptions tend to mark out the enuretic child as different from the non-enuretic child (Butler *et al.*, 1994). The two issues may be addressed as follows:

- *Frightened* – usually this represents a fear of being discovered as a bedwetter. It is important to renew the child's strategies for keeping it secret. Most children invest considerable effort

SELF IMAGE

Name . . . .

How would you describe yourself?

	Not at all				Very much so		
	0	1	2	3	4	5	6
1. Kind							
2. Friendly							
3. Confident							
4. Happy							
5. Lively							
6. Helpful							
7. Honest							
8. Tidy							
9. Feel different from others							
10. Lazy							
11. Lonely							
12. Stubborn							
13. Moody							
14. Worrier							
15. Nervous							
16. Shy							
17. Easily upset							
18. Frightened							
19. Bad tempered							
20. Angry							

Figure 6.3. The Self-image scale.

SELF IMAGE

Name . . . .

How would you describe yourself?

	Not at all					Very much so	
	0	1	2	3	4	5	6
1. Kind					■		
2. Friendly						■	
3. Confident						■	
4. Happy					■		
5. Lively						■	
6. Helpful						■	
7. Honest						■	
8. Tidy				■			
9. Feel different from others					■		
10. Lazy			■				
11. Lonely			■				
12. Stubborn	■						
13. Moody		■					
14. Worrier		■					
15. Nervous		■					
16. Shy		■					
17. Easily upset		■					
18. Frightened					■		
19. Bad tempered			■				
20. Angry	■						

Figure 6.4. A typical self-image profile.

in preventing the bedwetting becoming public knowledge. There are examples of siblings living in the same house being unaware of a child's bedwetting. Some children avoid holidays, camps, staying over at friends and so forth, yet as discussed earlier, there are ways to help children participate in such activities without the bedwetting becoming public. Some, at a later date, even avoid marriage so a prospective partner does not discover the 'dreaded secret'.

Many children (and parents) are too embarrassed to seek the advice of the family doctor or other health professionals, or to admit to the problem during screening interviews and surveys. It may therefore be a problem more prevalent in the population than surveys tend to suggest.

Children doubtless feel reassured when the knowledge is contained within the family. They are trusted not to break the secret, and although siblings may threaten to broadcast the bedwetting, this appears rarely to happen. A child will anticipate that were others, especially peers, to find out about the bedwetting, he/she would be singled out, ridiculed and perceived of as immature. As one child said 'If school knew, they'd tease me to death'. The fundamental threat to the child is that no longer would he/she be accepted for the many attributes he/she currently shows, but suddenly and pre-emptively as a bedwetter. No longer would the child be considered athletic, sensible, foolhardy, but as a bedwetter, and nothing but a bedwetter.

Taking care over who knows about the bedwetting therefore becomes crucial. Wagner and Geffken (1986) found, however, that 48% of children indicated a close friend's awareness of the bedwetting, suggesting it may be a problem willingly shared with trusted others. Shared secrets can represent a powerful dimension of friendship. Andrea illustrated this positive aspect of sharing secrets: 'My two best friends know I wet the bed. I talk with Emma. It helps when I talk about it. Secrets are fun. I like telling secrets to friends and they tell me their secrets'. The sharing of secrets involves personal investment and increased bonding between friends because it is based on a trust of each other.

• *Feel different* – because in general there is little difference between children with and without enuresis, a child can be reassured. Additionally, when children become aware of how prevalent bedwetting is, the sense of being alone with the problem can reduce dramatically. One method of enabling children to acknowledge this is to ask him/her how many other children in the school class might also suffer with bedwetting. Most children will say none. Figure 6.5 helps to make the point that according to prevalence figures, in a class of about 28–30 children, at 7 years of age, there will be at least another three children regularly wetting. Even at 10 years of age there will be at least one other child regularly bedwetting. Such information invariably inspires children

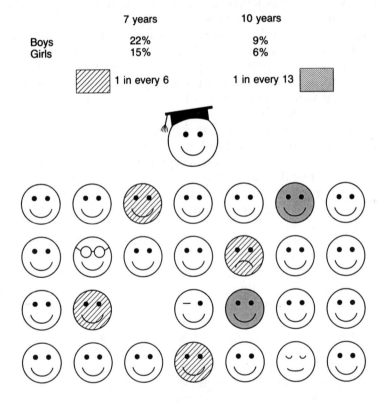

Figure 6.5. According to Rutter *et al.*'s (1973) prevalence figures, the probability of children with nocturnal enuresis in a school class of 28 children.

SELF IMAGE

Name . . . .

How would you describe yourself?

	Not at all					Very much so	
	0	1	2	3	4	5	6
1. Kind					▓		
2. Friendly				▓			
3. Confident			▓				
4. Happy			▓				
5. Lively			▓				
6. Helpful					▓		
7. Honest				▓			
8. Tidy				▓			
9. Feel different from others							▓
10. Lazy				▓			
11. Lonely						▓	
12. Stubborn				▓			
13. Moody							▓
14. Worrier						▓	
15. Nervous					▓		
16. Shy						▓	
17. Easily upset						▓	
18. Frightened							▓
19. Bad tempered						▓	
20. Angry				▓			

Figure 6.6. A self-image profile with high score on the negative descriptions.

to guess who it might be, an exercise which demystifies the uniqueness for the child.

It is sometimes the case that the Self-image Profile will indicate a child scores consistently highly on the negative (9–20) descriptions, as in Fig. 6.6. This is of concern because high negative self-image scores predict drop out from alarm based treatment (Butler *et al.*, 1994). As already discussed in Chapter 5, drop-out is regularly a consequence of maternal intolerance and it is worth speculating that a child's negative image and parental intolerance are related. Frude (1991) and Moffatt (1993), for example, both suggest punitive (intolerant) families lead children to blame themselves and suffer with lower self confidence and self esteem.

Both the self-image profile and maternal tolerance scale can therefore be employed to detect patterns predictive of drop out from treatment. The interventions taken when such patterns emerge are discussed in Chapter 5.

Perceived family attitudes

Cohen (1975) has emphasized the importance of determining the child's perception of the family. Butler (1987) presents an open ended method for gauging the child's view, and suggests the notions of support and/or tolerance often marks the child description. A structured means of eliciting the child's impression is given in Fig. 6.7. The child is asked to include all family members along the top row and check off (✔) who (if anyone) responds in the way indicated in statements 1–10 following a wet bed. The statements are derived from the factor analysed tolerance scale (Butler *et al.*, 1993) and represent five items indicating tolerance (1–5), and five items indicating intolerance (6–10). The results from *n*=50 children suggest:

- Mothers are generally viewed as more tolerant *and* intolerant compared with fathers. In particular they are more inclined to be perceived as:
  Tolerant
  i.   Recognizing the child can't help it (mother 91%; father 74%).

FAMILY ATTITUDES

Name: . . . .   Family members

After a wet bed:	Mum	Dad						
1. Who feels sorry for me (F3)								
2. Who thinks its a pity it stops me from doing so many things (F3)								
3. Who tries to help me not to be upset (F6)								
4. Who recognizes I can't help it (F5)								
5. Who says it doesn't matter (F1)								
6. Who shows their disappointment (F1)								
7. Who thinks it is a nuisance (F4)								
8. Who feels I don't try hard enough (F4)								
9. Who thinks I should grow up a bit (F2)								
10. Who punishes me/teases me (F2)								

Figure 6.7. Family attitudes.

ii.   Helping the child not be upset (mother 86%; father 50%).

Intolerant
iii.   Thinking it is a nuisance (mother 57%; father 34%).

iv. Thinks child should grow up a bit (mother 38%; father 21%).

- Mothers are viewed as *more* intolerant than how mothers think of themselves.
- Over half the children (58%) say they are teased by their siblings because of the bedwetting, a finding similar to previous results (Butler, 1987).

Seeking the child's view of parental attitudes helps compose a picture of family dynamics and with whom the child feels supported. Where lack of support is evident (lack of checks on tolerant items) the child may feel isolated and rejected. Where intolerance is suggested there will be an immediate need to work with the family in restructuring support for the child, and developing interventions to quickly resolve the bedwetting.

Children's efforts

In response to what has been tried to help overcome the bedwetting, one boy retorted 'learnt to swim'. Perhaps humorous, yet the response also reflected perplexity about his inability to curb the bedwetting. Asking children about their attempts to overcome the problem is revealing. Figure 6.8 indicates some varied replies, prompted by logic, ingenuity, myth and parental caprice. A survey of attempts found the most common child generated methods were changing fluid intake, toileting more frequently and alteration of the sleeping pattern (Butler, 1987), not dissimilar to measures parents tend to adopt.

Both Wagner and Geffken (1986) and Butler (1987) discovered a sizeable minority (13–14%) noted they had done 'nothing' to try and achieve dry nights. This perhaps suggests a group of children who have not resolved *why* they should become dry, and it may be hypothesized that these are the children who would be unresponsive to treatment at this stage.

Albert Einstein once remarked 'imagination is more important than knowledge.' Some children display a remarkable faculty for invention in solving their problem. One boy considered jogging as a solution because it would rid him of the excess water through perspiration. Another boy sought to discover

Figure 6.8. Children's attempts to overcome bedwetting.

themes in the pattern of his bedwetting and set up a form of experiment to test his predictions – 'when I'm ill I don't wet, so I try to get a bit of a cold – not so's I'm ill but just a bit.' These boys, inventive and eager to participate in the solution to their difficulties, were at the stage of challenging *how* they could become dry. They were prepared to anticipate themselves as being free of wetting, and the offer of help with the enuresis alarm was readily greeted with enthusiasm and success.

A more structured approach to the exploration of children's efforts can be achieved with the chart illustrated in Fig. 6.9. This invites the child to:

i.   recount what might have been attempted, under the six headings;

ii. comment on the effect, or what difference each effort made. Interestingly, most reflections focus on the detrimental effects;

iii. through discussion, work out approaches which build on the child's efforts but offer a greater chance of success. Thus much of what is discussed with parents concerning fluid intake, toileting and not lifting can be reinforced with the child. Here is also the opportunity to seek out what problems the child has accounted with previous use of the alarm, and how they might be rectified.

Problematic implications

Possibly one of the most important questions to ask of children concerns the issue of what might be difficult, disadvantageous or problematic about the possibility of becoming dry. An enquiry about the good aspects of continuing to wet or the bad things about becoming dry will make little sense to many children, and will be greeted with a perplexed expression. However, occasionally a child will volunteer a notion which makes bedwetting seem meaningful or which goes a long way to resolving some further problem. In such instances the bedwetting is not perceived as a problem, but a *solution* to some other problem. Some examples given by children where bedwetting serves as a solution are as follows:

EFFORTS TO OVERCOME BEDWETTING

Name . . . .

What have you tried	What difference did it make	What might be improved
1. Change of fluid intake _____ _____ _____	_____ _____ _____ _____	_____ _____ _____ _____
2. Toileting _____ _____ _____	_____ _____ _____ _____	_____ _____ _____ _____
3. Sleeping pattern changes _____ _____ _____	_____ _____ _____ _____	_____ _____ _____ _____
4. Alarms _____ _____ _____	_____ _____ _____	_____ _____ _____
5. Medication _____ _____ _____	_____ _____ _____ _____	_____ _____ _____
6. Other: _____ _____ _____	_____ _____ _____ _____	_____ _____ _____

Figure 6.9. Efforts to overcome bedwetting.

- Pleasure – 'its warm': 'see steam coming out'.
- Preserves a particular relationship with parents – comfort; contact; support, all of which is threatened by becoming dry.
- Resists adulthood/maturity – avoids responsibility: continued dependence.
- Achieves special status – bedroom for self.
- Avoids 'unwanted' social engagements – overnight stay with relatives.
- Controls others' behaviour – 'stops mum coming in to my room and telling me to tidy up'.
- Achieves a need – missing school to come to the clinic.
- Avoids unpleasant events – 'stops the dog sleeping on my bed': 'the smell stops burglars breaking in'.
- In situations where the child is being abused sexually.

These examples imply that for the child there is an advantage in continuing to wet the bed, and until the issue is resolved the child will resist becoming dry. Research bears this out. Where children express any advantage for continued bedwetting the chances of failure in traditional alarm treatment are greatly increased (Butler *et al.*, 1994). Therefore the fundamental problem needs to be addressed prior to assisting the child to find ways of overcoming bedwetting.

Inviting children to explore their bedwetting through discussion, structured questions and formats can be illuminating to both child and clinician. It may offer the child an alternative perspective. Occasionally this by itself may resolve the issue and assist the child to discover an alternative stance towards the bedwetting or feel supported in attempting new interventions. Sometimes a 'spontaneous recovery' occurs following such an interview. Usually it serves to demonstrate to the child that his/her notions are taken seriously and the clinician will offer support and encouragement throughout the struggle to achieve bladder control.

7

Understanding the problem

The human crisis is always a crisis of understanding:
what we genuinely understand we can do
Raymond Williams

The format of an initial interview is paramount. Time, patience and perceptiveness spent on understanding and differentiating the problem will have untold rewards in enabling an appropriate intervention or programme to be designed. To do otherwise often leads to trial and error efforts, dispirited children and frustrated parents.

An interesting metaphor for the first interview with parent(s) and child is that of a research supervisor and research students (Bannister and Fransella, 1986). The research students, in this case, mother and child, each present at the first meeting a thesis in which they are the only informed experts on a situation they are personally involved. The supervisor (clinician) is an expert only in as much as he/she is more conversant with bedwetting in a wider, more general sense.

Usually, however, it is the child who perceives him/herself as the focus of the interview. He/she is the reason for their presence together. For some children this feels threatening, especially where great lengths have been taken to avoid other people learning of their problem. The child is after all, giving licence to the discussion of something very personal and potentially embarrassing. Some children are therefore satisfied to withdraw, remain reticent and leave the discussion to adults.

Inevitably some areas are dominated by parents, although as the interview flows and weaves through many aspects, there are points where the child should be encouraged to contribute. Children feel less intimidated when the clinician is perceived as relaxed, concerned for the child, ready to listen and able to offer assistance. Acceptance of the child – his hopes, ambitions, dislikes, enjoyments and so forth – irrespective of the bedwetting, is also helpful. Thus we begin to see, and enable the child to see, that he/she is not just a bedwetter, but rather, a child who is confronted with a difficulty, that of bedwetting. This view may be considered propositional in that it tempts us to see the child from a broad perspective. This avoids the restricting encounter where the child is viewed as nothing but a bedwetter, and where our interests are concerned only with the bedwetting.

The interview is considered to have both a philosophy, where each person is considered an expert in the field and where all contributions are therefore valued; and a function, that of assessment, where problems are elaborated and interventions designed. Fielding and Doleys (1987) are also of the opinion that a too simplistic approach without regard to appropriate assessment may serve to overlook subtle features and thereby contribute to prolonged treatment, drop out, failure and relapse.

The initiative for structuring initial interviews comes from the clinician who may rely on a framework to elicit the relevant information. The rest of this chapter focuses on some of the salient aspects which are discussed in relation to their implications for treatment. A structured format for collecting the relevant information is provided by Butler (1993c).

Sex of child

Table 7.1 highlights the different profile presented by girls. Rutter *et al.* (1973) have gone so far as suggesting two varieties of enuresis based on the sex differences. They propose a monosymptomatic developmental disorder of boys, and a disorder in girls associated with behavioural problems and daytime bladder difficulties. With girls the treatment implications may involve:

- Analysis and examination of possible stress factors.
- Assistance in helping parents manage the associated behavioural difficulties.
- Addressing the daytime difficulties of bladder control.

Table 7.1. Important characteristics for girls with enuresis which differentiates them from boys.

- Less common in early childhood (Fielding, 1980)
- Irregular prevalence pattern across ages with 'peaks' at 7 yrs, 10 yrs and 14 yrs (Verhulst *et al.*, 1985)
- Less evidence of a genetic aetiology (Bakwin, 1971)
- More likely to have secondary enuresis (Rutter *et al.*, 1973)
- Associated daytime wetting is more common (Jarvelin *et al.*, 1988)
- Daytime frequency is more common (De Jonge, 1973)
- More likely to have associated emotional and behavioural problems (Rutter *et al.*, 1973)
- Mothers are more tolerant of enuresis (Butler *et al.*, 1986)
- Mothers are more likely to worry (Foxman *et al.*, 1986)

Age

- Children should be encouraged to recognize the high incidence of nocturnal enuresis across all ages, and consequently that they are not alone with the problem. In Chapter 1 the prevalence and chronicity of nocturnal enuresis was discussed.
- Most clinicians agree on the need for minimal intervention below 5 years of age (Weir, 1982), but alternative criteria other than age may be regarded as more relevant, such as how severely the bedwetting is interrupting social, emotional, cognitive or motor development (Cohen, 1975) or the degree to which the bedwetting is a concern to parent and child (Butler, 1987).
- Spontaneous remission of around 14–16% a year, (in boys) for nocturnal enuresis can be expected (Forsythe and Redmond, 1974).

Family structure

- *Size*: Rutter *et al.* (1973) found a slight, though insignificant and inconsistent, tendency for nocturnal enuresis to be more common in children from large families. Oppel *et al.* (1968b) found more relapses following successful treatment to come from large families.

- *Membership*: It is important to grasp the family composition and members of the household, particularly when some treatments such as an alarm may demand parental assistance, or where maternal intolerance suggests the need to involve other members in supporting the child.
- *Child's position*: This involves delineating the birth order and discovering the child's perception of his position, e.g. the eldest responsible child or the youngest with licence to remain immature. It is also relevant to discover if any siblings also suffer or suffered with nocturnal enuresis and why the present child has been identified as the one requiring help.
- *Maternal loss*: Absence of a father, through separation, divorce, death or being an unmarried mother does not appear to be associated with the presence of nocturnal enuresis (Tissier, 1983). However maternal loss or recurrent separation from the mother during a child's early years seems related to the occurrence of nocturnal enuresis (Douglas, 1973; Jarvelin *et al.*, 1990).
- *Disruption*: Dische *et al.* (1983) define this as serious marital discord or parental mental illness and showed children in such families were less responsive to alarm based treatments. On a similar theme, Young and Morgan (1973a) found mothers with a tendency to anxiety, were associated with slower progress in alarm based treatment.
- *Family history of nocturnal enuresis*: Up to 70% of children with nocturnal enuresis have a parent who suffered in a similar way (Bakwin, 1971). It is as yet indiscernible, as discussed in Chapter 3, how much the vulnerability to nocturnal enuresis is transferred genetically or environmentally. Thus a family with parents who were themselves enuretic might hold different expectations for their children than parents who were not themselves enuretic as children. This is one of a number of possible environmental variables that might influence whether a child from an 'enuretic family' has a greater chance of being enuretic.

Wetting history

- *Removal of nappy*: The age at which nappies were removed

and rationale given by parents might suggest something of their stance. Some parents have inflexible, directive attitudes and remove the nappy when they believe the child ought to be dry. Other parents respond to the child's indication of wanting to be dry. It is of course probable that some children upwards of 5, 6 or 7 years of age wear nappies, and because this may provide the child with 'a licence to wet', it is good practice to negotiate the removal as quickly as possible.

- *Occurrence of dry nights*: MacKeith *et al.* (1973) suggest that the achievement of even 1 dry night indicates that maturation of the necessary mechanisms involved in bladder control has occurred, and a month of dry nights suggests maturation is complete.

- *Longest period remaining dry: Persistent* (or primary) nocturnal enuresis describes those children who have yet to demonstrate an extended period (usually for 6 months) of dry nights. In contrast, where children have experienced being dry for an extended period, prior to the occurrence of regular night-time wetting, the term *onset* (secondary, regressive or acquired) enuresis has been used. Dische *et al.* (1983) suggest the period of dryness should be at least 1 year, and this has been acknowledged by the American Psychiatric Association DSM III criteria (1980). The risk of onset enuresis appears heightened where:

  i.   The child attains bladder control after 5 years. Fergusson *et al.* (1990) suggest there is a 3½ times greater chance of onset enuresis with such children compared to those achieving bladder control before 3 years of age. Late age of acquiring bladder control might therefore be considered to be the *vulnerability factor*.
  ii. The child is exposed to stressful situations or life events (Shaffer, 1980; Fergusson *et al.*, 1990; Jarvelin *et al.*, 1990). Such events might be considered the *provoking factors*.

Fergusson *et al.* (1990) demonstrated that where children experienced both factors – acquiring bladder control after 5 years and being exposed to four or more life events in a year – they were 8 times more likely to develop onset enuresis in that year compared to children acquiring bladder control before 3 years of age and who experienced no life event exposure. They postulate that persistent and onset enuresis represent 'two sides of the same coin'. On the one hand, the child's ability to acquire and maintain nocturnal bladder control is related to the rate at which control is acquired; on the other hand this capacity seems to play a role in the child's susceptibility to lapsing when exposed to stress (Fergusson *et al.*, 1990).

Because the rate of therapeutic response does not appear to differ between children with persistent and onset enuresis (Sacks and DeLeon, 1973), some writers (e.g. Doleys, 1977; Shaffer *et al.*, 1984) suggest the distinction may be irrelevant. However, there are some recent studies which suggest children with onset enuresis may well present a picture with different prognostic implications:

a. Onset enuresis at 9 years of age appears to predict later behavioural problems (Feehan *et al.*, 1990).
b. Children with onset enuresis are more likely to relapse following successful alarm treatment (Butler *et al.*, 1990b).

- *Frequency of wetting/week*: Palpably this illustrates the seriousness of the problem. The majority of children wet at least once a week (Verhulst *et al.*, 1985), although Butler (1991) argued that for research studies there should be an incidence of at least 50% wet nights over 2 weeks. As discussed in Chapter 1, other variables such as parental and child concern will justifiably influence the clinical decision regarding treatment interventions. It does seem *apparent* that children with *regular* wetting (every night) compared with *intermittent* wetting (occasional nights) find it more difficult to acquire nocturnal bladder control (Miller, 1973) and tend to be more prone to relapse following treatment (Lovibond and Coote, 1970).
- *Frequency of wetting/night*: Children wetting more than once a night are sometimes described as *multiple* wetters. They take significantly longer to become dry during alarm treatment and are also more susceptible to later relapse (Finley *et al.*, 1982; Houts *et al.*, 1986).
- *Pattern of wetting*: Rarely are patterns readily identified but for the very occasional instances they do occur they usually represent:

i.   a manifestation of stress – e.g. nights prior to returning to school after a weekend or holiday.
ii. a suggestion of altered sleeping patterns – e.g. sleeping late on a Sunday morning.

In Chapter 12 (Fig. 12.5) a detailed record chart is illustrated which can suggest possible routes to examine in assessing for regular patterns.

• *Spontaneous waking*: The occurrence of spontaneous waking indicates a developing awareness of bladder signals. The child's behaviour following waking is interesting to follow. Three types of response tend to occur:

1. Toileting (entirely appropriate).
2. Reluctance to leave the bed to toilet because of the cold, a fear of the dark or a fear of monsters (emotional avoidance).
3. An unwillingness to leave the bed to toilet because of the effort involved (motivational avoidance).

Interventions to encourage the child to toilet might include a torch, a landing light left on or a receptacle in the room (for emotional reasons) or a strategy of incentives for successful toileting (for motivational reasons).

Wetting behaviour

The definition of nocturnal enuresis includes a statement relating to the involuntary nature of the micturition. The number of children who wet deliberately (voluntarily) are negligible (Morgan, 1981), and cannot be classified as suffering with nocturnal enuresis.

Such children do, however, deserve attention and assistance but require interventions of a different nature. It is important to differentiate voluntary acts of micturition from nocturnal enuresis. The following are some examples of voluntary micturition (Butler, 1987):

– a 9-year-old girl urinated on the carpet next to the bed. Her mother placed a plastic mat by the bed which the girl

subsequently jumped over and again found the carpet to urinate on. This continued for a number of nights with mother placing increasingly more plastic mats on the carpet, and each time the girl found a spare piece of carpet to urinate on.
– An 8-year-old boy gouged a hole in the wall and proceeded to urinate into the cavity wall insulation.

Other acts of what appear 'voluntary' urination such as micturition in to a fish tank, plant pot or wardrobe may be either a consequence of the child's fear of leaving the room and finding a 'safe place' in which to urinate, or a failure to completely wake as a result of a full bladder, and without being conscious enough to visit the toilet, voiding occurs in an inappropriate situation.

Consequences of wetting

- *Does the child come into the parents bed*? Christmanson and Lisper (1982) discovered 25% of children who would later become bedwetters had been taken into the parents' bed following a wetting episode. This compared with only 3.5% of non-bedwetters and suggests parental actions in allowing the child to complete sleeping in the parents' bed reinforce the continuance of bedwetting.
- *Who cleans up*? It is informative to find out who is involved in stripping and remaking the bed, laundering and drying the bedding. This will provide clues as to the involvement of other family members, the extent to which the child is left to 'make good' himself and a flavour of the parental attitude towards the child.
- *Do any punitive actions follow*? White (1971) and Butler (1987) suggest a third of mothers admit to being punitive towards children who bedwet. It is important to determine the degree of and severity of such actions which might range from verbal reprimands, removal of privileges and threats, to physical punishment. The appropriate interventions where parents show intolerance of enuresis are examined in Chapter 5.

Associated problems

- *Daytime wetting*: Between 10 and 28% of bedwetting children have daytime bladder difficulties (Forsythe and Redmond, 1974; Pierce, 1980), and are often referred to as *mixed* wetters. Such children seem more resistant to treatment of the bedwetting (Fielding, 1980; Bollard, 1982) and more prone to relapse following alarm treatment (Lovibond and Coote, 1970; Fielding, 1980). It is good practice to tackle the day wetting prior to commencing a treatment programme for bedwetting. Types of day wetting are illustrated in Table 7.2 with urge incontinence being the most common cause of mixed enuresis (Schmitt, 1982). Meadow (1990) has comprehensively described the problem of day wetting on its own, with two-thirds of these children reportedly wet by day being reliably dry at night.

Elaboration of the problem can be achieved by determining the presence of the following:

a. *High frequency* of toilet visiting – up to seven voids a day is considered normal (McKendry and Stewart, 1974), and a high frequency indicates a difficulty in holding large quantities of urine, thus suggesting low functional bladder capacity (Fielding, 1982).

b. *Difficulty in holding* (postponing micturition) – the sensations of urgency are usually perceived early enough for the child to postpone urination until a toilet is reached. Swithenbank *et al.* (1993) suggests asking the child whether they need to leave a school lesson to use the toilet, or are unable to wait to the end of a television programme, are helpful in deciding on the presence of urgency. Swithenbank *et al.*'s (1993) sample suggested 70% of boys and 62% of girls who wet the bed reported no urgency, yet Fielding (1982) found for those children with mixed wetting, 86% had urgency. Urgency is indicative of possible problems in bladder signal recognition or awareness.

c. *Postures to prevent urination* – Fielding (1982) observed a range of postures from crossing legs to foot jogging in order to overcome the feelings of urgency. These *overt* bodily signs of urgency can be used by parents to both prompt the

Table 7.2. Types of daytime wetting.

• GIGGLE MICTURITION (sudden, involuntary wetting with giggling, laughing, tickling or excitement)	– mostly present in girls – may clear during adolescence – use of stop-start exercises may be helpful
• URGE INCONTINENCE (intense bladder spasms leading to abrupt voiding)	– most common in girls – most common variety of day wetting – may have lifelong history of urgency and frequency – high incidence of UTI – use regular toileting as treatment routine
• STRESS INCONTINENCE (wetting as a result of coughing or sneezing)	– rare in childhood
• TRANSIENT WETTING (infrequent wetting episodes)	– usually stress related or with UTI – most common in younger children – equal across boys and girls – stress reduction techniques needed or easy access to toilet (school)
• CARELESS WETTING (wetting whilst absorbed in play)	– use regular toilet routine or developing body cues as a signal for bladder sensations
• CONTINUOUS DAMPNESS	– suspicion of ectopic ureter and need for medical screening
• OVERFLOW INCONTINENCE (straining on urination, dribbling)	– possible lower urinary tract obstruction (rare)
• RESISTIVE WETTING (child resists using the toilet)	– often boys – avoid punitive, restrictive or inflexible reactions from parents – reward success

child to use the toilet and assist the child to recognize them as signals for the need to use the toilet.

d. *Large volumes of urine passed* (polyuria) – this signals the need for more extensive medical investigation, as would the presence of *painful urination* (dysuria), and difficulty in *starting urination* (hesitancy). Dysuria with frequency and the sudden onset of daytime wetting indicates the presence of UTI (Schmitt, 1982).

e. *Returning quickly to the toilet within a few minutes* – this is suggestive of residual urine and again requires medical investigation.

f. *A stop-start urine stream* – the presence of a non-continuous urine flow suggests dysfunctional voiding with a lack of co-ordinated response between bladder and urethra, where the pelvic floor muscles rather than relaxing during voiding, tend to contract. Such occurrences require urological investigation with biofeedback as a means of establishing a co-ordinated response.

- *Encopresis*: There are a number of types of soiling problems (Rutter, 1976), the most usually associated with bedwetting being *constipation* which can irritate the bladder or inhibit the bladder emptying.

The child's lifestyle

- *Bedtime*: This should indicate the regularity of the child's sleeping pattern, with chaotic, irregular or very late bedtimes (related to the child's age) possibly affecting the body's rhythm and release of vasopressin.
- *Sleeping arrangements*:
  a. Shared room – Dische *et al.* (1983) suggest that sharing a room with more than one other child can adversely affect initial success with the enuresis alarm. The inconvenience an alarm presents to siblings has to be considered and encouraging them to support a treatment programme through assisting the child to wake, or share the rewards of success can be helpful. It may of course, if feasible, be worth considering a change in sleeping arrangements to allow the child with bedwetting to have a room to him/herself, be close to parents, or close to the toilet.
  b. Bunks – the ease of access to the toilet if the child sleeps on the top bunk requires investigating.
  c. Shared bed – if possible the introduction of an enuresis

alarm should be deferred until the child can have a bed to him/herself.

- *Availability of toilet*: There may be *physical* (e.g. attic bedrooms) or psychological (e.g. fear of the dark) reasons which make the child's access to the toilet during the night difficult.
- *Heating*: Kaplan and Sadock (1982) suggest bedwetting occurs in cold rooms more than better heated rooms, and is also more prevalent in winter compared with summer.
- *Sleeping away from home*: Many children will remain dry for the first few nights sleeping in unfamiliar circumstances away from home. Parents sometimes interpret this as an indication that something is wrong or detrimental to the child at home. Morgan (1981) suggests this is not the case and argues that in addition to being more sensitive and aware of external cues (e.g. noises) when sleeping in unfamiliar situations, the body's awareness of internal cues (e.g. bladder sensations) is also increased. The phenomena can be used positively to emphasize the probability of remaining dry when the child elects to try sleeping at a friend's or go on a school trip overnight.

In summary, information is only important if it assists our understanding and influences decisions about the appropriateness of treatment interventions. Focusing on the variables contained within this chapter encourages a dialogue with both parent(s) and child which seeks to elaborate the uniqueness of the problem and lays the foundation for tailoring a treatment programme to meet their needs. The variables are:

- Sex of child.
- Age.
- Family structure.
- Wetting history.
- Wetting behaviour.
- Consequences of wetting.
- Associated problems.
- The child's lifestyle.

8

Promoting good practice

What deeply affects every aspect of a man's experience
is the perception that things could be otherwise
Michael Frayn

A challenge for professionals working with children with nocturnal enuresis must be to vigorously pursue improvements in service provision and delivery. Publication of the 'Guidelines on Minimum Standards of Practice' (Morgan, 1993) is a watershed in raising awareness of appropriate goals. The Guide presents 53 *minimum* standards and a framework of 30 loftier ideals described as *target* standards. Pursuit of such laudible objectives provides the hallmark of good practice and this chapter explores the means by which such aims can be achieved. They are covered under the following sections:

- Service delivery.
- Baseline measures.
- Pre-treatment predictors.
- Involving the child.
- Effective treatment interventions.
- Outcome measures.
- Treatment predictors.
- Consumer acceptability.

Service delivery

Efficient services might be considered those which reach the appropriate population and provide assistance as immediately as possible. This statement suggests a need to explore:

i. the population;

ii. the way of reaching them;
iii. the provision of immediate access.

(i) *Population*: the Guide suggests this is *limited* by the following parameters:

- A geographical boundary or catchment area;
- Any prioritizing of referrals which should relate only to the child's age, clinical presentation or treatment practicality.

and should *not* be limited by:

- the child's place of residence whether at a boarding school or children's home;
- the child's gender, race, culture, socio-economic background, nationality, history of being in care, or religious belief.

(ii) *Reaching the population*: this will be influenced by:

- The referer's knowledge of the service – the Guide suggests all potential referers need to be provided with regular and updated information about the nature of the service.
- The public's awareness of the service – this might be achieved through publicizing the service in public places such as libraries, health centres and other community facilities.
- The parent/child's ease of access – Young and Morgan (1972a, b) report that drop out from treatment is exacerbated where parents find difficulty in attending clinics. After school clinics might further improve accessibility for working parents and/or children who feel embarrassed at missing school to attend regular clinical appointments.

(iii) *Provision of immediate access*: the Guide outlines the following minimum and target standards in relation to this:

- Waiting time between referral and first appointment – 3 months (minimum); 1 month (target).
- Waiting time at clinic to be seen – within 30 minutes (minimum); within 15 minutes (target).

Baseline measures

The waiting time before an appointment can be gainfully used, by sending the parent/child the following:

- Some information about the nature of the problem.
- A chart to encourage the child to record the frequency of wetting.

Such involvement encourages families to 'opt in' to treatment rather than drop out because their involvement is recognized and they have taken a decision to invest some of their energies in to the recording of their behaviour. A baseline chart (Butler, 1993c) may invite the child to record the following for each night over a 2- or 4-week period:

- number of drinks per day;
- the presence or absence of a drink before bed;
- the occurrence of a wet night.

Thus at the first appointment the chart will reveal the severity of bedwetting and the presence of any fluid restriction. It can also be 'eyeballed' for progress, as a small minority of children will achieve bladder control during this exercise, as a consequence of increased awareness and feedback of results, and indeed spontaneous recovery can be up to 15% per annum (Forsythe and Redmond, 1974). A baseline may also be scanned for patterns and will provide a record against which the effectiveness of any consequent treatment intervention can be measured (Butler, 1987).

Pre-treatment predictors

Table 8.1 illustrates a variety of factors identified as being responsible for decreasing or inhibiting the child's chances of success with an enuresis alarm. The presence of such variables during an initial assessment should enable the clinician to mould a more appropriate treatment intervention at the outset. Particular cognizance should be taken of:

Table 8.1. Pre-treatment factors which predict outcome with alarm treatment.

	Drop out (early withdrawal)	Failure	Relapse
Practicalities			
transport difficulties	Young and Morgan (1972 b)		
previous unsuccessful alarm	Young and Morgan (1972 c)	Fielding (1985)	
longer period on a waiting list			
Housing			
unsatisfactory		Dische et al. (1983)	
Family			
positive family history	Young and Morgan (1972 a)	Dische et al. (1983)	Dische et al. (1983)
family discord		Devlin and O'Cathain (1990)	
family stress			
maternal intolerance / anger	Morgan and Young (1975) Wagner et al. (1982) Butler et al. (1988) Wagner and Johnson (1988)		
Child			
negative self image	Geffken et al. (1986) Butler, Redfern and Holland (1994)	Butler, Redfern and Forsythe (1990a)	
positive implications behavioural difficulties	Geffken et al. (1986) Wagner and Johnson (1988)		
socially withdrawn		Wagner et al. (1982)	Sacks and DeLeon (1978)
Wetting			
secondary enuresis			
multiple wetting	Fielding (1980)	Fielding (1980, 1982) Houts (1992)	Butler, Brewin and Forsythe (1990b) Finley et al. (1982) Young and Morgan (1973d) Fielding (1980) Bollard (1982)
associated daytime wetting			

- Child and family variables which predict drop out (maternal intolerance, a child's negative self image and behavioural difficulties): this might be an occasion for the employment of medication which relieves the problem transiently, enables the parent to feel better, improves the child's self confidence and keeps the family attending appointments (Butler, 1993a).
- Associated daytime difficulties, multiple wetting and history of secondary enuresis which increases relapse: the daytime problem might be tackled first (Houts, 1991). Adjuncts to the enuresis alarm such as retention control training (Fielding, 1982) or extended supervision and monitoring (Bollard and Nettelbeck, 1982) might be suggested possibilities.
- The indications of failure:

  - Unsatisfactory housing: Dische *et al.* (1983) suggest alarm treatment might be delayed where there is an absence of an indoor toilet or the child sharing a bedroom with more than one other child. If more appropriate sleeping arrangements cannot be negotiated, the employment of medication might be indicated.
  - Previous unsuccessful alarm use: great care should be taken in presenting alarm treatment again. However, it is the case that alarm treatment is more successful with older children (Butler *et al.*, 1990c) so a second 'go' is not out of the question. Alternative alarms (e.g. body warm or vibrator alarms) are also available for the child's choice, but it is essential to ensure the child understands the reason for employing an alarm, is clear about the instructions and is committed to having another go.
  - Family difficulties: alarms with a silent (vibrating) signal might reduce the distress of other family members waking to an audible alarm. It may be important to emphasize the child's active role (see below) in achieving success. Where family stress is a reaction to the child's enuresis, the role of medication might again prove crucial.
  - positive implications for remaining wet (the child who resists becoming dry because the bedwetting solves some other problem). Here the bedwetting is not a problem but a *solution*. It may serve to protect the child from sexual abuse, preserve a relationship with parents which the

child perceives as being threatened by becoming dry, or avoid other unpleasant events. Alarm treatment in this context is unlikely to succeed because it fails to resolve those issues which maintain the bedwetting. The underlying problem needs addressing prior to helping the child deal with the bedwetting.

Involving the child

Liberman (1978) suggests a fundamental element in the effectiveness of many diverse therapies is the ability to engage the client's sense of mastery. This may be accomplished by:

- Enhancing the child's understanding of bladder functioning and control, using illustrations and metaphors appropriate to the child's age to describe bladder filling, signals of fullness and the need to recognize such signals. When children acknowledge that such signals need to be brought to their awareness, alarm treatment can be readily introduced as a method for assisting the child to recognize bladder signals.
- Involving the child in decisions over treatment strategies. This may include:

  - Exploring hypotheses the child may have about the way to become dry, e.g. incentive schemes, types of drink.
  - Discussing the child's efforts and building on or adapting their initiatives.
  - Exploring the viable treatment options and encouraging the child to select those which best meet his/her needs.
  - Provide a choice of different types of alarm system for the child when opting for alarm treatment.

Such efforts involve children creatively in their own treatment (Noll and Seagull, 1982). Where children have this sense of involvement and autonomy in the treatment process they are committed to it and, in a very real sense, engineer their own success. Clinicians who independently analyse the problem and alone select the treatment, violate the child's involvement and desire to succeed. The child remains a passive recipient rather than an active and enthused ingredient.

- Foster the child's responsibility, by addressing two aspects in particular:

  - The encouragement of independence by, as far as the child is able, engaging him/her in setting up the alarm (when used), keeping records, diaries and charts and participating in changing the bedclothes and sheets.
  - The promotion of ownership where the child feels a treatment intervention is individually designed to meet his/her needs.

Effective treatment interventions

Good practice must be underpinned by interventions with a proven record of effectiveness, and a history of rigorous scientific testing. To advocate less is selling the child short. This does not rule out intuitive or innovative ideas provided they are based on sound theoretical notions, tailored to the child's needs and elected by the child as a favoured option. Effective interventions should:

- prove better than a spontaneous rate of 15% a year (Forsythe and Redmond, 1974);
- have minimal side effects (Fitzwater and Macknin, 1992);
- compare favourably with response rates from alternative interventions.

The enuresis alarm meets these criteria, and has consistently been found to be the most effective intervention in helping children cease bedwetting. Johnson (1980) reviewed early *uncontrolled* studies of the enuresis alarm (where no comparison groups were examined). Of 23 such studies, 17 included children treated as out-patients, and amounted to a total of 1684 individuals. The results suggest the bedwetting alarm realized:

- Up to 40% *drop out*, with a range from 0 to 40%.
- A good rate of *initial success* with 35–100% of the total sample reaching the criteria for success.
- Nine studies quoted over 90% success and half the studies reported over 80% initial success.

- *Relapse* ranged up to 56% (Freyman, 1963; Turner and Taylor, 1974).

Three reviews of *controlled* studies (alarm compared with other treated or untreated groups) have been undertaken:

1. Doleys (1977) – reviewed 12 studies between 1965 and 1975 with 808 children.
2. Johnson (1980) – reviewed 14 studies between 1955 and 1977 with 640 children.
3. Forsythe and Butler (1989) – reviewed 26 studies between 1938 and 1989 with 1525 children.

The consensus of opinion from these reviews is:

- The enuresis alarm is more effective than no treatment controls or other forms of intervention. Table 8.2 presents the results of comparative studies.
- Using the author's own criteria the enuresis alarm is effective in helping children to cease bedwetting in 65–75% of cases.
- The duration of treatment averages around 5–12 weeks before initial success is reached.
- Up to 40% of children will relapse within 6 months of treatment.

Table 8.2. Studies comparing the enuresis alarm with control groups.

Enuresis alarm more effective than:
- no treatment controls – Collins (1973), Bollard and Nettelbeck (1981)
- placebo – Turner *et al.* (1970), Wright and Craig (1974)
- waking non-contingently – Young (1964), Baker (1969), McConaghy (1969), Turner *et al.* (1970)
- delayed alarm triggering – Collins (1973), Peterson *et al.* (1969)
- medication – Blackwell and Currah (1973), Wagner *et al.* (1982), Houts *et al.* (1992)
- psychotherapy – Werry and Cohrssen (1965), DeLeon and Mandell (1966)
- retention control training – Fielding (1980), Geffken *et al.* (1986).

Reviews are, however, necessarily handicapped by the variety of methodologies and definitions of outcome employed in individual studies. Early studies seldom relied on objective criteria but chose terms such as 'improved' and 'temporarily favourable' or vague and questionable definitions such as 'stopped altogether or having occasional accidents' (McKendry et al., 1972).

Outcome measures

The lack of criteria and widespread confusion between 'accepted' definitions prompted an exhaustive appraisal of the literature culminating with a proposed set of *working definitions* of outcome measures (Butler, 1991). Although principally suggested as a framework for research studies to aid comparison, the working definition give focus, precision and goals to accomplish in clinical practice.

As Houts *et al.* (1992) persuasively argues, outcomes reported for interventions with medication (pharmacological therapies) usually refer to *reductions in wetting frequency* compared with outcomes for alarm treatment which typically report percentages of children who *cease bedwetting*. Such different outcome measures make comparisons between alarm based and medication based interventions difficult, and almost meaningless. Houts *et al.* (1992) proposes that the difference may reflect dissimilar objectives, with pharmacological therapies emphasizing *management* of enuresis (and thus reports of reduced frequency makes sense), whereas, in contrast, alarm based treatment stress the achievement of bladder control (with reports of numbers who cease bedwetting making sense).

The agreed set of working definitions are outline in Table 8.3.

- *Initial success* – this requires the consideration and fulfilment of two specifications:

    - an extended number of dry nights (14);
    - within a specified treatment duration (16 weeks).

- *Lack of success* – by implication this appertains to those not meeting the initial success criteria. It also excludes those

Table 8.3. Working definitions of outcome measures. From Butler, R. J. (1991) *Archives of Disease in Childhood*, **66,** 267–271.

Initial success	Achievement of 14 consecutive dry nights within a 16 week treatment period
Lack of success	Failure to meet the initial success criteria excluding drop outs
Drop out	Following an initial appointment, two consecutive appointments are missed without notice *or* treatment is discontinued by agreement of parent, child and therapist
Relapse	More than 2 wet nights in 2 weeks
Continued success	No relapse in the 6 months following initial success
Complete success	No relapse in the 2 years following initial success.

cases which withdraw prematurely from treatment.

- *Drop out* – this category, in theory, should cover all cases which do not fall in to the first two (initial success and lack of success). It is thus something of a mixed bag. The working definition describes *when* a case might be categorized as drop out but does not indicate *why* the child/parent/therapist might terminate treatment prematurely.

The reason for drop out could indeed locate the case in any category. Thus early withdrawal might be a result of:

☐ Success – e.g. the parent/child might consider further appointments unnecessary when the child achieves lengthy spells of dry nights. Indeed Young and Morgan (1972a) found 19% of children stopped treatment prematurely because they had become dry.

☐ Failure – e.g. a reluctance to attend appointments when the treatment interventions show little sign of being effective. Young and Morgan (1972b, c) found lengthy time to initial arrest a predictor of drop out. Further, cases of drop out 'failures' might include those where the family or therapist decide to discontinue treatment because of lack of progress.

☐ Unavoidable withdrawal – e.g. where extraneous factors intervene to make the continuation of treatment difficult or impossible. Such cases represent valid drop out and should be omitted from any calculations of success rates. Examples might include moving away from the area, sudden disruption in the family structure (e.g. a death in the family) or the treatment intervention breaking down (e.g. the alarm failing).

- *Relapse* – only a small number of children will remain completely free of bedwetting episodes once treated (Dische *et al.*, 1983), and therefore a degree of 'slippage' can reasonably be construed as acceptable. Additionally, occasional bedwetting occurs amongst 'non-enuretic' children and bladder control is remarkably vulnerable during times of illness or stress. Dische *et al.* (1983) argue that such lapses of control tend to remit spontaneously and do not predict further relapse. Making allowances for occasional accidents complicates the working definition. It focuses on:

  - the duration of monitoring, once treatment is terminated;
  - the elapsed time over which wet nights are observed (2 weeks);
  - the number of wet nights (more than 2).

- *Continued success* – nearly all relapses occur within the first 6 months following treatment (Dische, 1973; Sacks and DeLeon, 1983; Forsythe and Redmond, 1974; Dische *et al.*, 1983). Thus regular monitoring of progress for 6 months after initial success is considered good practice. Where relapse does not occur, then a case can be described as continued success.
- *Complete success* – relapses are less common after 6 months, and thus less intensive monitoring for up to 2 years has been advocated. Complete success describes those children who do not relapse within 2 years of their initial success.

The Guide on Minimum Standards (Morgan, 1993) advocates the keeping of outcome data, utilising the working definitions. The recommendations include a formula for evaluating the effectiveness of a service, which might be calculated annually, and used for audit and decisions regarding improvements to the service.

The formula:

Single effectiveness indicator = $\dfrac{\text{No. of success}}{\text{No. of children treated}} \times 100$

Treatment predictors

Once a treatment programme is established some variables appear to predispose the child to failure or early withdrawal from treatment. These are outlined in Table 8.4. Clinicians need therefore to be ever vigilant of such factors, and take remedial action when required. Salient factors include:

- *Lack of supervision* – The Guide (Morgan, 1993) suggests:

    - following the start of treatment, follow-up should be within 1 week (if only by telephone);
    - subsequent contact should be maintained at 2 to 3 week intervals;
    - arrangements are put in place whereby assistance can be provided between appointments when necessary.

- *Lack of cooperation* – Johnson (1980) has suggested the majority of those who fail with alarm treatment can be considered to be non-compilers. Sometimes, of course, it might be parents who resist alarm usage because of broken nights and difficulty in getting children back to sleep. Most issues concerning cooperation and compliance should be picked up during the assessment stage, and provided the principles of involving the child, and tailoring treatment to the child and family needs are adhered to, the number of cases of non-co-operation should be minimized.
- Issues with alarm based treatment – Table 8.4 displays a range of variables which can interfere with treatment, which will be explored in Chapter 9.

Table 8.4. Features of treatment which predict adverse outcome

	Drop out (early withdrawal)	Failure	Relapse
Lack of supervision	Dische (1973) Bollard and Nettelbeck (1981)	Goldstein and Book (1983) Houts (1992)	Bollard and Nettelbeck (1981)
Lack of cooperation with treatment	Young and Morgan (1972 a) Houts et al. (1986)	Doleys (1977) Forsythe and Redmond (1970) Taylor and Turner (1975)	
Lengthy time to initial arrest	Young and Morgan (1972 c)		
Alarm based treatment:			
– Child's fear	Young and Morgan (1972b)	Forsythe and Redmond (1970)	
– Failure to wake	Young and Morgan (1972a)	Young (1965) Taylor and Turner (1975)	
Unreliability of alarm	Azrin and Theines (1978)		
Inconsistent use of alarm		Collins (1973) Forrester, Stein and Susser (1964)	

Consumer acceptability

The Guide (Morgan, 1993) draws attention to the importance of evaluating the service from the child's and parent's perspective, and employing the information to plan and update the future delivery of service. Butler (1993c) provides a consumer satisfaction form to gauge the parents' opinion of the service. This form seeks to understand how far the standards set by the Guide are perceived as being met by the parent, and are elaborated in greater detail in Chapter 12.

9

The enuresis alarm

Comments are free, but facts are sacred
C. P. Scott

The origins of alarm treatment date back to 1830, when Nye first suggested the possibility of waking children at the onset of wetting (Glicklich, 1951). A German physician called Pfaundler, in the early part of the century, realized the potential of an alarm system when he utilized a device, in a hospital setting, to alert nursing staff to bedwetting episodes so that the bedding could be changed. To his surprise he discovered that the frequency of children's wetting episodes decreased dramatically. The idea was born.

However, it was Mowrer and Mowrer (1938), some years later, who placed the bedwetting alarm on a theoretical base, and it is they who are generally recognized as the architects of alarm treatment.

The alarm consists of a sensing device which detects the 'leakage' of urine, upon which an alarm is activated to awaken the child. At the same time the alarm causes contractions of the pelvic floor muscles and thus the inhibition of urination. Upon waking the child is encouraged to finish voiding in the toilet.

The alarm system has now become the *'treatment of choice'* because of its demonstrable record of effectiveness (see Chapter 8). A number of different forms are manufactured (see Appendix A) with some recent designs showing dramatic reductions in size and which can be worn attached to the child's bedclothes. Wagner *et al.* (1982) suggest all models operate according to the same principles, with recent designs perhaps showing a greater acceptance amongst the children who use them.

The essential principle of the alarm system is to alert and

sensitize the body to respond quickly and appropriately to a full bladder during sleep (Butler, 1987). More specifically, Baller (1975) suggests the notion behind the alarm is one where the threshold tension of the detrusor is converted from being a signal of urination to being a signal for the *exact opposite response* – that of inhibition of urination and waking.

Theoretical interest focuses on how the alarm converts the meaning of the signal from one of urination to one of hold-ing/waking. Mowrer and Mowrer (1938) advocated a classical conditioning paradigm, proposing that bodily reactions (pelvic floor muscle contractions interrupting urination) become ap-propriately associated with the sensation of a full bladder.

There are, however, problems with the assumption upon which this paradigm rests. Because the alarm is activated *after* urination begins, pelvic floor contractions and inhibition of urination is associated with a bladder less than maximally full. Quite how the transition 'backwards' to full bladder sensations evoking holding and waking, rather than urination, is not adequately explained (Yates, 1975).

Aspects of alarm treatment which may contribute to effec-tiveness include:

- *The development of avoidance*: Triggering of the alarm by uri-nation produces a series of 'aversive' consequences for the child. These might include *sensations* (the loud noise of the alarm, feeling wet, adapting the eyes to light on waking, feeling cold on waking); *increased activity* (disturbed sleep, toileting, changing wet sheets) and detrimental effects on the child's emotions and self image (disappointment, inade-quacy, perceived parental intolerance).

  The alarm can be construed as if it were an aversive stimulus which the child seeks to find ways of avoiding. Where the child responds to a full bladder by waking or contracting the pelvic floor muscles and holding, he/she avoids the unpleasant consequence and remains dry. Lovibond (1964, 1972) termed this a *conditioned avoidance response* which is reasonably resistant to extinction or re-lapse. A child may, however, discover ways to avoid the noise of the alarm through inappropriate means. This might include:

- not arousing but sleeping through the alarm;
- failing to set up the alarm or switch it on prior to sleep;
- switching off the alarm and returning to sleep without toileting when it is triggered.

Such responses are considered later but serve to emphasize the importance of engaging the child in treatment through ways which increase the child's understanding and commitment (see Chapter 8).

- *The development of increased functional bladder capacity*: Houts (1991) suggests that one mechanism of action may be the conditioning of pelvic floor contractions in response to bladder filling, a response which inhibits urination and may enable increased volumes of urine to be stored in the bladder, enabling the child to sleep through the night without urination. Troup and Hodgson (1971) noted the relationship between alarm treatment and increased functional bladder capacity.
- *The increased production of ADH (anti-diuretic hormone)*: Given that increases in serum vasopressin are known to occur as a physiological response to stress, Houts (1991) speculates that suddenly waking from sleep because of an alarm may result in increased levels of endogenous ADH over the course of alarm treatment. As discussed in Chapter 3, release of ADH reduces urine production so the child is enabled to sleep through the night without the bladder capacity being exceeded.
- *The alteration of social and motivational factors*: Azrin *et al.* (1973, 1974) suggest a large component of the effectiveness of alarm treatment arises because it brings about the arrangement of social influences in an optimal way. Parental reactions and the child's annoyance at waking are scheduled to occur at the time of wetting (and therefore potentially more effective) rather than in the morning, as happens without the alarm. Reactions to wetting in the morning have a minimal chance of being effective because the consequences are too remote from the point at which wetting occurred.
- *Increased expectancy*: Broken alarms, or alarms not switched on, have been shown to help some children reduce the frequency of bedwetting episodes. The hope and anticipation of becoming dry are enhanced in the context of clinical

appointment, child orientated interviews, use of progress charts, feedback of results, praise for doing well, and the gadgetry of an enuresis alarm.

The following processes might therefore be identified as influential when an enuresis alarm is employed:

- The child's expectancy of success is enhanced.
- The alarm produces an interruption of urination, which may lead to increased capacity to hold and ability to sleep through the night.
- On waking the stress may increase ADH production with decreases in urine volume.
- On waking a number of aversive consequences (social and practical) follow in close proximity to the bedwetting.
- The child discovers alternative responses to full bladder sensations, other than urination, which appropriately would include holding or waking to toilet, or may inappropriately lead to sabotage of the alarm system.

The remainder of this chapter focuses on the following aspects of the bedwetting alarm:

- Description of the system.
- Suitability.
- Recommended procedure.
- Effectiveness.
- Trouble shooting.

Description of the system

Several firms in the United Kingdom manufacture enuresis alarms (see Appendix A), of essentially three types: bed alarms (with detector mats on the bed); body worn alarms; and integral alarms, all based on the same principle of alerting the child at the point of urination.

Bed alarms

Often referred to as the *pad and bell*, bed alarms adhere to the

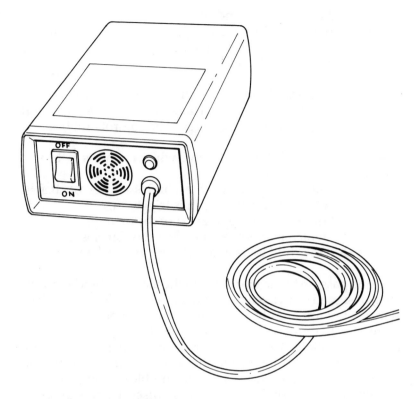

Figure 9.1. Eastleigh SMI alarm.

original design of Mowrer and Mowrer (1938), and can be described with reference to one of the most widely used alarms, the Eastleigh SMI illustrated in Fig. 9.1. The alarm consists of:

- *A foil embossed plastic mat* placed on the bed which detects urine. It is arranged in the following way:

  - A waterproof sheet over the mattress.
  - The mat placed where the wetting is likely to occur.
  - A top sheet to cover the mat, preferably of thin cotton to allow urine to soak through quickly.

A mat can deteriorate very quickly. To avoid this it:

- should be kept clean and dry;
- when not in use during the day, stored under the mattress to keep flat. This also keeps it out of sight of inquisitive visitors to the bedroom.

- *A control unit* which should ideally be placed away from the bed to encourage the child to leave the bed and switch it off (and subsequently visit the toilet). The control unit has:

  - a lead, divided at the distal end, which connects to the two studs of the detector mat;
  - an on/off switch, which the child switches on before sleep, and off when the alarm is triggered;
  - a test button to check operation of the battery;
  - a light which is switched on when the alarm is triggered to alert the child to its whereabouts in a darkened room.

Urine passing to the mat triggers the alarm, a discontinuous tone, designed to awaken the child quickly. The loudness of the alarm is not apparently a critical factor, the noisiest being no more effective in awakening the child (Young and Morgan, 1973c). Essentially it is the child's recognition of the importance of the alarm signal, not the loudness, which brings about waking. However, some alarms provide audible options, such as a constant tone or variable frequency of pulses. There are sockets on some control units to provide for attachments, the main ones being:

  - A vibrator unit, placed under the pillow, or on the bedhead, which when triggered produces movement to waken the child. These prove useful for children who have difficulty waking to an audible alarm, children with a hearing impairment, or those sleeping in a dormitory.
  - An extension alarm to reach the parents' bedroom if they need to help a child who for example might be physically disabled.
  - An audible awakener to increase the noise of the alarm.

Body worn alarms

These are small electronic alarms worn pinned to the pyjamas

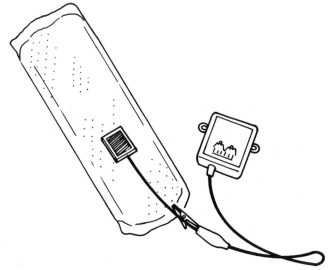

Figure 9.2. Malem Night Trainer.

and connected by wire to a small urine sensitive detector placed in an absorbent disposable pad worn inside the underwear (Fordham and Meadow, 1989; Butler *et al.*, 1990c). Figure 9.2 illustrates the Malem Night Trainer alarm.

Immediately the child begins to urinate, the detector is moistened, which triggers the audible alarm. The principle remains identical to that for the bed alarm, where alarm triggering at the onset of urination leads to pelvic floor muscle contractions with inhibition of urination, and waking.

Body worn alarms have some advantages over bed alarms:

- They have *face validity* – because the sensor detects the beginning of urination immediately, it is often the case that the child is wakened before the bed becomes wet. This has distinct advantages for the child who is not confusingly faced with the paradox inherent with bed alarms, i.e. you have to wet the bed for it to stop you wetting the bed. With the body worn alarm, children can be persuaded to use it because it will keep the bed dry even during the learning phase of developing bladder control. The case of dry beds

also is very persuasive with parents who are otherwise faced with the excesses of wet sheets.
- They *avert*, to some degree, *sabotage* because the body alarm has no on/off button. This means the child, provided he/she puts it on before retiring to bed, cannot 'forget' to switch it on, or cannot turn over and switch it 'off' without the sensor pad first being dried.
- They have *consumer acceptability* – children prefer body alarms to bed alarms because of the size, portability and comfort (Butler *et al.*, 1990c).

Integrated alarms

A development from the body worn alarm has been the introduction of a 'wireless' system, once more adhering the same principle of the other two systems. The sensor is permanently attached to the alarm box which in turn is clipped to the child's underwear. The alarm is illustrated with the Simcare Goodnight alarm (Fig. 9.3). This alarm seeks to improve upon the body worn alarm by:

- Abandoning the idea of a disposable pad which boys in particular find off-putting. It is replaced with a washable cloth pouch covering the sensor strip.
- Having two cues – audible and vibration movement – to wake the child.
- Encouraging the child to complete voiding in the toilet (rather than turning over and returning to sleep) once the alarm is triggered, by having a magnetic key (which switches it off) held by the toilet (Butler, in preparation).

What the three types of alarm system offer is *choice*: for both clinician and child, a notion in accord with the principles outlined in the Guide on Minimum Standards (Morgan, 1993).

Suitability

Enuresis alarms continue to be used successfully with children from 4 years upwards, with both boys and girls responding equally well. Although regarded as the 'treatment of choice',

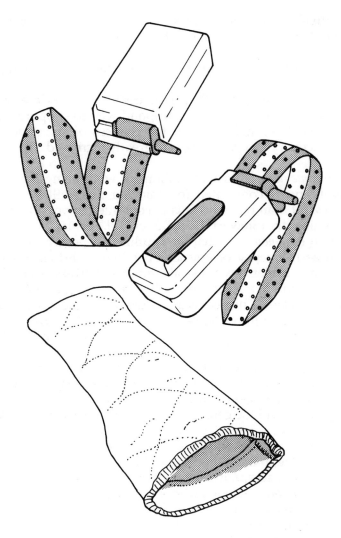

Figure 9.3. Simcare Goodnight Alarm (integrated alarm).

some parameters need to be observed when considering the employment of an enuresis alarm:

* *Age.* Many examples can be found of alarms being used

effectively with children under 7 years of age. However this can only be advised with great care because:

(i) The risk of frightening a child is increased the younger he/she is.
(ii) It might be argued that alarm treatment is too intensive given younger children respond well to support plus incentive, and also that the chances of spontaneous recovery at a young age are greatly increased.

- *Commitment.* A child with notions of what being dry will entail, and is committed to achieving this, will be more successful than one who fails to construe the possibility of becoming dry (Stewart, 1975; Butler *et al.*, 1990a).
- *Wetting behaviour.* As Chapter 8 outlined, aspects of wetting such as frequency of episodes per night, and associated daytime problems will reduce initial effectiveness and increase future relapse (Fielding, 1980; Finley *et al.*, 1982).
- *Intellectual level.* This seems unrelated to treatment outcome, except with children with learning difficulties who may need to have reached a cognitive level commensurate with a 7-year-old before the alarm is utilized.
- *Stress.* It seems axiomatic to avoid times of transient stress such as family disruption, moving house or changing schools because of both the difficulty of establishing a regular pattern, and the consequent emotional upheaval for the child.
- *Parental cooperation.* Ideally parents need to be enthusiastic, encouraging, patient (because of the lengthy time to initial success) and accept involvement in treatment.
- *Home situation.* A single bedroom is not a necessity. Siblings initially woken by an alarm will often habituate to the sound because it quickly assumes little importance for them. Occasionally siblings will, however, wish to assist and encourage the child with waking and support.
- *Children in residential settings.* Disruption caused by the alarm in terms of disrupted sleep was considered by Jehu *et al.* (1977) to be hardly discernible in a children's home. However, the jibes that can follow the knowledge of a child's use of an alarm can quickly resonate throughout the community. It may be advisable in care provision, boarding

schools or residential homes to carefully judge the climate before employing an alarm, even of the non-audible type.

Recommended procedure

Presentation

As far as possible this should be orientated towards the child and presented in a climate conducive to success. The alarm remains the child's responsibility (Meadow, 1977; Butler, 1987). McKendry and Stewart (1974) emphasize the necessity of the child's active participation and parents' enlightened inactive concern.

For younger children the alarm might be introduced as an electronic ally serving to keep the child informed of his bodily needs. Further, the child might respond to a competitive invitation to try and beat the alarm triggering (i.e. waking before the alarm sounds) just as they might strive to beat a friend at running or other sporting venture.

With older children, Morgan (1981) inspired the analogy of acquiring a new skill, emphasizing that all children are good at some things and not so good at other things. Being not very adept at bladder control is just as common as not being very good at, say football, or playing the piano. The way to improve is through coaching/teaching the technique. With regard to bladder control the clinician takes such a role and may employ an enuresis alarm to increase the child's awareness of bladder fullness and the appropriate skills – holding and/or waking – to achieve the possibility of staying dry.

Instructions

Dische (1973) and Turner (1973) have discussed in depth the necessity of written instructions and demonstration. The alarm needs setting up in the clinic for the child to understand and test. Morgan and Young (1973b) feel few children are fearful of an alarm if it is fully demonstrated to them. Children also need the space to ask questions. For the clinician it is good practice to explore the degree of adjustment required within the family in coping with the alarm. One pertinent question for the child relates to what problems he/she might anticipate in using the alarm. In this way the child's fears, lack of clarity and uneasiness can be addressed prior to employing the alarm.

Written instructions and advice come with all alarms and manuals for parents and children are now readily available to assist in understanding the various aspects of alarm usage. Appendix D provides details of such manuals.

Following a routine helps the child establish appropriate reactions to the alarm. One such routine might be:

- A small drink (avoiding diuretics, such as tea and coffee) in the last hour before bed.
- A toilet visit prior to switching the light off.
- Using the alarm consistently every night, with breaks allowed for illness or visitors staying at the child's home.
- A parental check at their bedtime to ensure the alarm is appropriately set up and/or switched on.
- On triggering the alarm, the child should:

  - Quickly switch the alarm off. Where the child sleeps through the cue, a parent needs to intervene rapidly and wake the child, so he/she can switch it off. Collins (1976) described a game whereby child and parent compete to switch the alarm off – the first to do so earning a point, with a cumulative score kept to decide a winner.
  - Visit the toilet to complete voiding.
  - Remove the wet sheets and remake the bed, a procedure sometimes referred to as *cleanliness training*.
  - Re-set the alarm in cases where multiple wetting is likely to occur.

A child might familiarize him/herself with a routine through a dry run. This will involve a practice at home of the various stages of the routine with the alarm triggered with a little salty water. Detector mats and sensors require cleaning in the morning with a damp cloth. Sheets require washing before re-use (with bed alarms), otherwise perspiration in contact with dried residue of urine may trigger the alarm falsely.

Removal of the alarm should be contingent on an agreed number of consecutive dry nights – usually 14 (Butler, 1991), although sometimes children choose to keep the alarm in the room or in place and not switched on as a 'reminder' before going to bed. Following initial success, the following aspects require covering:

- Follow-up visits: as discussed in Chapter 8 these will be required for a time, as relapse, if it occurs, is likely to happen within the subsequent 6 months.
- The possibility of occasional wet nights: these might arise as a result of stress, illness or tiredness and can be treated as 'blips' or 'one-offs'. Dische *et al.* (1983) found only 16 of 55 children successfully treated did *not* have an occasional accident, but these cleared up spontaneously.
- The need for contact if occasional wetting episodes increase in frequency: where wetting episodes begin occurring at the rate of 2 or more a week, the family should be encouraged to consult the clinician quickly to avert the possibility of complete relapse.

Effectiveness

As Chapter 8 documented, alarm treatment has become the 'treatment of choice', because in comparison with other interventions it has consistently demonstrated greater evidence of success in enabling children to become dry.

Investigating the merits of different alarm systems remains in its infancy. The available evidence suggests:

- Bed alarms, body worn alarms, and integrated alarms all demonstrate *equality in terms of effectiveness*. The survey by Forsythe and Butler (1989) reviewed 26 studies of the bed alarm with an average 68% success; and six studies of the body worn alarm with an identical initial success rate. Later comparison work between all three systems (Butler *et al.*, 1990c; Butler, in preparation) suggests there is little to separate them with regard to the percentage of children who initially acquire dryness.
- Body worn and integrated alarms are superior to bed alarms in the *time it takes to achieve initial success*. Butler *et al.* (1990c) and Butler (in preparation) found bed alarms took on aver-

age approximately 8 weeks to achieve success [consistent with Doley's (1977) survey], whilst body and integrated alarms take on average about 5 weeks for the child to reach the initial criteria. This makes perfect theoretical sense. The body and integrated alarms are triggered immediately urination begins, whereas the bed alarm is reliant on urine seepage through to a bed mat before triggering. Thus the consequences (pelvic floor muscle contraction, inhibition of urination, and waking) occur much closer in time to the sensations of bladder fullness, and therefore the learning process (avoidance or association) should be expected to be more rapid.

Troubleshooting

Failure to wake to the alarm

Perhaps the most frequent source of dissatisfaction is the child's lack of arousability on alarm triggering, which may lead to parental annoyance and decisions to abandon such interventions. This is also the strongest factor associated with a slow response (Young and Morgan, 1973a). The best solution is prevention.

Prior to the first night ensure:

- The child fully understands the *purpose* and what he/she should do when the alarm is triggered.
- The need for *speed* (quickness of response) is understood.
- The child grasps the idea that if he/she is *prepared* to wake, when the alarm triggers, the chances are that he/she will do. The issue is one of ensuring the alarm signal is construed as important, and a self instruction something like 'If the alarm goes off I will wake' can prove important in preparing the child prior to sleep.

Should non-waking persist, then a number of alternatives suggest themselves:

- Introduce a system to increase motivation such as 'beat the buzzer' when the child receives points/stars for

waking quickly or before the alarm is triggered (spontaneous waking).
- Advising parents to help the child wake up, but encourage the child to switch the alarm off. For a while it may be advisable for a parent to sleep in close proximity to the child so the speed of response can be quickened.
- Offering a different alarm system.
- Changing the alarm signal. Young and Morgan (1973c) discovered that children respond to different characteristics of an alarm, the loudest not necessarily being the most effective. Some alarm systems have varying audible signals (pulsed or continuous); others offer additional assistance with vibration as a signal
- Reinforce waking (see arousal training in Chapter 11).

Failure of alarm to trigger

Most usually this will be caused by a run down of the battery. With bed alarms, the inadvertent use of a nylon sheet might prevent urine penetration.

False alarms

These can prove both frustrating and irritating for the child, and the most likely reason is perspiration:

- Reduce bedclothes.
- With bed alarms ensure the sheets are laundered to remove stale urine.
- With body worn alarms cover the sensor with cotton wool if a pad is not worn.
- With integrated alarm keeping the cloth pouch laundered should prevent false alarms.

Failure to urinate after awakening

The tendency to switch off or remove the activated alarm and return to sleep is forever present, but reduces the alarm's potential effectiveness because toileting is evaded. Possibilities of avoiding such actions and encouraging the child to complete voiding in the toilet are:

- Bed alarm: placing the control box as far from the bed as possible so the child is required to leave the bed to switch it off
- Body worn alarm: placing an incentive in the bathroom so the child is encouraged to visit the toilet.
- Integrated alarm: the key to switch the alarm off can be kept by the toilet.

10

Facilitating the alarm

If a child fails to learn in the way we teach, can we teach in the way he learns Harry Chasty

The ubiquitous alarm! Accepting the premise that the enuresis alarm is the 'treatment of choice', can incline the clinician towards inflexible stereotypical 'off the shelf' treatment packages. Such action fails to do justice to the child's unique experience, the context within which the bedwetting happens, and the child's available resources to tackle the problem. The alarm may prove to be the fundamental tenet of a treatment programme, but a successfully designed programme will be tailored to meet the child's needs. Many alternative interventions have been proposed and tested, either to stand on their own, or dovetailed into a structured programme. Perhaps the best known of such programmes are Dry Bed Training (Azrin *et al.*, 1974) and Full-Spectrum Home Training (Houts and Liebert, 1984), both of which employ the alarm and when vigorously tested it is the alarm which proves to be the most effective component of such packages (Bollard and Nettelbeck, 1982; Houts *et al.*, 1986).

Alternative strategies and interventions might therefore be re-framed and considered as adjuncts to the alarm, selected to meet a particular need but employed alongside an alarm to facilitate the child's progress toward the achievement of bladder control.

The various adjuncts have been discussed in depth by Butler (1992) and can be categorized as in Fig. 10.1. Each adjunct will be discussed using a format for easy reference:

- A rationale, or principle underlying the method.
- A description.
- Some variations taken from the literature.

Customary routines	Bladder training
• cleanliness training • active responsibility • counselling/support	• retention control training • sphincter control • bladder stretching

Arousal techniques	Cognitions
• positive practice • waking schedules • self awakening • waking by association	• auto suggestion • re-structuring beliefs • visualization

Intake	Incentives
• diet/fluids • overlearning	• arousal training • rewards • reward and penalty

Figure 10.1. An array of adjuncts to possibly employ with the alarm.

- Effectiveness.
- When to use.

Customary routines

Cleanliness training

Rationale

- To increase the child's *awareness* of the inconvenience of wetting.
- To involve the child in *taking responsibility* for the accident and restoring the situation 'as new'.

Description (from Azrin et al., 1974)

- Following the detection of a wetting episode the child is encouraged to complete voiding in the toilet.
- The child is then required to remove night clothes and wet sheets and place them in the laundry.
- The detector mat/sensor requires cleaning and drying by the child.
- Clean sheets and night clothes should be obtained and the alarm re-set by the child.

Variations

- Almost all authors now suggest the child's involvement in some or all aspects of cleanliness training is good practice.

Effectiveness

- The study by Bollard and Nettelbeck (1982) suggested cleanliness training did not add significantly to the alarm's effectiveness.

When to use

- Cleanliness training has become almost a routine adjunct to the alarm, but modified in relation to the following factors:

    - The child's age, with younger children not expected to complete the full procedure without assistance from parents.
    - Because Bollard and Nettelbeck (1982) suggest the procedure can be construed as aversive, it is wise to emphasize that the child's involvement in cleaning up is not a punitive response.

Active responsibility

Rationale

- To foster the feeling that children have control over their behaviour – that they can be *instrumental in changing* aspects of their behaviour.

- To encourage children to be *active participants* rather than passive recipients.

Description (adapted from Marshall et al., 1973)

- Encourage the child to keep a chart of factors which might influence a wetting episode (e.g. going to bed late, worrying about school).
- Discuss with the child how control might be exerted over such parameters.
- Enhance awareness of the sensation of a full bladder by

  - Holding before urination.
  - Describe to him/herself the feelings this evokes prior to urination.

- Stop-start during urination can emphasize the child's power to control urination.

Effectiveness

- Marshall *et al.* (1973) report such a procedure to be as effective as the alarm or medication, although they fail to report the number of children who achieved a dryness criteria.

When to use

- With older children (8 years +), as effectiveness improves with age.
- To prevent relapse. Marshall *et al.* (1973) report relapse rates as low as 5%.

Counselling/support

Rationale

- To *allay* the child's anxieties and unease.
- To encourage the child's *responsibility*.
- To *reduce parental anxiety*.

Description (from White, 1971)

- Reassure the child regarding the commonness and treatability of wetting.
- Provide an explanation of the reasons for wetting – demystification of the problem.
- Demonstrate and emphasize that wetting is not the child's fault, through illustrations and/or metaphor.
- Encourage the child to record dry nights with a smiling face or star, and ask that this be brought to the clinic for the next appointment.
- Praise the child for whatever progress is made.
- Fluid intake is not restricted, which facilitates a supportive relationship between child and clinician.
- Parents are asked to look for improvement, and show pleasure for dry beds.
- Parents are asked not to comment on wet beds and refrain from any punitive measures.
- The child is reassured he/she is not alone with the problem – the likelihood of another child in the same class at school having the same struggle is highly probable.

Variations

- Assuring parents of the commonness of the problem (see Chapter 1).
- Have a record chart which invites the child to draw a picture for each morning he/she wakes with a dry bed. Dische (1971) reports that such drawings tend to become bolder as the child's confidence in being dry increases.
- Remove any guilt the child may have by stressing the inherited vulnerability to wetting amongst family members (Schmitt, 1982).
- Use of manuals to help reassure the child and involve him/her in exercises to overcome the problem e.g. 'Eric's Wet to Dry Bedtime Book' by Butler and Parkin (1989), 'A Guide for Teenagers' by Dobson (1991).
- Involve the child in choosing between treatment options.

Effectiveness

* White (1971) and Dische (1971) both report success with such support. Dische (1988) reported 10–20% respond by use of this method alone.

When to use

* With younger children particularly.
* With children in need of reassurance.
* The supportive ethos is important with all children.

Bladder training

Retention control training

Rationale

* To assist the detrusor muscles in *adapting* to increased bladder pressures and volumes.
* To *increase functional bladder capacity*.
* To enable the child to *sleep through* the night without needing to toilet.
* To *sensitize* children to bladder sensations.

Description (from Fielding, 1980)

* One session a day.
* Following urination the child is encouraged to drink 500 ml of fluid.
* The child is subsequently invited to wait as long as possible before a further visit to the toilet.
* As the child indicates a need to void, note the time (or start a stopwatch).
* Encourage the postponement of toileting or voiding for as long as possible.
* When he/she cannot hold any longer, encourage the child to void into a measuring jug.
* Note the time between first indication and voiding.
* Praise for holding.

- Employ a chart to monitor time of postponement and volume of urine voided.
- At each subsequent session, ask the child to postpone urination for an additional 1–2 minutes.
- Praise increases in postponement times and voided volumes.
- Graph the increases against time to demonstrate progress.

Variations

- Holding may be undertaken at the toilet door – holding initially for 5 seconds and increasing postponement times by 5 seconds for each successful trial.
- Use of incentives and rewards to increase holding (Paschalis *et al.*, 1972; Houts *et al.*, 1986).
- At the juncture the child indicates a need to use the toilet, a set holding time (such as 5 minutes) can be suggested, a time which can be increased in intervals (e.g. 3 minutes) for three consecutive trials, and to a maximum of 30 minutes (Doleys *et al.*, 1977).
- Azrin *et al.* (1974) incorporated *one* intensive training night in the Dry Bed Training programme, which involves hourly awakening, the choice to toilet or hold until the next hourly awakening and encouragement to drink each hour.

Effectiveness

- Up to 40% success (with an undefined criterion of success) has been claimed where RCT is used on each occasion the child wishes to void (Paschalis *et al.*, 1972).
- The general finding is an *increase in functional bladder capacity* but *without the desired reduction in bedwetting* (Doleys *et al.*, 1977; Harris and Purohit, 1977).
- RCT fails to *produce improvement in day or night wetting* for children with mixed enuresis (Fielding, 1980).
- RCT proved *not to be an effective component* of Dry Bed Training (Bollard and Nettelbeck, 1982), possibly because it was undertaken on only 1 night.
- The addition of RCT to alarm treatment has been found to *improve response time* for children with small functional bladder capacities (Geffken *et al.*, 1986).

- The addition of RCT to alarm treatment does *not appear to prevent future relapse* (Houts *et al.*, 1986).

When to use

- Age 7+.
- When there is evidence of small functional bladder capacity, e.g. daytime frequency, multiple wetting at night.

Sphincter control

Rationale

- To *strengthen control* of the external urethral sphincter and the pelvic floor muscles controlling bladder neck descent.

Description (from Bennett et al., 1985)

- Help the child understand that the procedure aims to strengthen bladder muscles so they remain contracted and keep the bladder 'water tight' during sleep.
- At least once during daytime toilet visits the child is requested to stop the flow of urine, count up to three and begin voiding again for a further count of three.
- The procedure may be repeated up to six times a toilet visit.

Variations

- The stop-start exercises have been incorporated into retention control training (Doleys *et al.*, 1977) and daytime dry bed training (Azrin and Theines, 1978).

Effectiveness

- Generally this method has proved unsuccessful when used on its own, with less than 20% reaching success (Bennett *et al.*, 1985), a figure no better than spontaneous recovery.

When to use

- Only with children over 7 years of age.

- In situations where the child shows evidence of stress incontinence or weak sphincter muscles, but not with bladder instability.

Bladder stretching

Rationale

- To *prolong intervals* between daytime voidings.
- To *increase functional bladder capacity*.
- To enable the child to *sleep through the night* without the need to urinate.

Description (from Starfield, 1967)

- Increase daytime drinking, either by providing the child's favourite drink or salty foods such as crisps or peanuts.
- Time the gaps between urination.
- Encourage the child to hold for longer periods of time.
- Encourage the child to resist the urge to urinate for as long as possible.

Variations

- Focus on the sensations accompanying a full bladder at the point of urination.
- Urinate once a day into a measuring jug to monitor progress (Schmitt, 1990).
- Set time limits (such as every 2 hours) between urination and when these are achieved, increases can be determined.

Effectiveness

- Up to 35% success within 6 months has been claimed by Starfield (1967) although no success criteria were documented.

When to use

- Over 7 years of age.
- Where there is evidence of daytime frequency or small functional bladder capacity.

Arousal techniques

Positive practice

Rationale

- To *mass practise the desired response* of waking and toileting.
- To strengthen the appropriate response as *an alternative* to bedwetting.

Description (from Azrin et al., 1974)

- A practice trial involves the child:

  - lying on or in the bed with lights out;
  - counting to 50;
  - arising and attempting to urinate in the toilet;
  - returning to bed;
  - repeating this procedure 20 times.

- Such massed practice is scheduled to occur:

  - on the discovery of a wetting episode;
  - before going to bed on the following night.

Variations

- The counting may be reduced to 20, and repetition schedules to 10 for younger children (Butler *et al.*, 1988).

Effectiveness

- Positive practice proved to be one of the least effective components of the full dry bed training programme (Bollard and Nettelbeck, 1982).
- It is essentially perceived as aversive and raises objections from both child and parent (Bollard and Nettelbeck, 1982; Griffiths *et al.*, 1982).

When to use

- Children over 7 years of age.
- With highly motivated children and parents who do not construe it as punitive.
- With children who show a high resistance to waking.

Waking schedules

Rationale

- To encourage the *waking response*.
- To encourage urination in the *appropriate place*.
- To ease *arousability from sleep*.

Description

- The success of waking schedules depends on:

  - ensuring the child is completely awake (thus counteracting the problem of toileting without waking which reinforces nocturnal enuresis);
  - facilitating irregular waking times (to avoid routine bladder emptying at specified times).

- These principles have been inculcated into a number of waking schedules:

  - random;
  - scheduled;
  - staggered;
  - intensive.

1. Random waking (from Young, 1964)

- A random predetermined schedule of waking times is agreed upon, at which time the child is woken.
- The child may be involved in the selected times by having 6 scheduled times (whereupon the roll of a dice before bed determines the time for that night e.g. Butler, 1992).

2. Scheduled waking (from Azrin et al., 1974)

- Three hours after falling asleep the child is woken fully and asked to toilet.
- Following a dry night the child is woken ½ *hour earlier* the next night (i.e. the waking is brought forward).
- After a wet night the waking remains at the same time as the previous night.
- The waking is discontinued when the interval between going to sleep and scheduled waking is 1 hour.

3. Staggered waking (from Creer and Davis, 1975)

- For 2 weeks the child is woken 3 times a night, the times being determined by the child drawing numbers from a hat.
- For the next 2 weeks the random times are reduced to 2 a night, and then to once a night after a further 2 weeks.
- Waking is stopped after a further 2 weeks.

4. Intensive waking (from Azrin et al., 1974)

- *One* night is selected as a training night, which should be at a weekend or holiday from school.
- The child is fully informed of the procedure so he/she is not suddenly confronted by the experience.
- After an hour of sleep the child is woken with minimal prompting.
- At the toilet door the child is asked whether he/she wishes to urinate or hold for a further hour.
- The child chooses to urinate or hold.
- The procedure is repeated *each hour* through the night.

Variations

- All procedures might be enhanced by:

  - praise for appropriate behaviour (waking, toileting, holding);
  - feedback to the child about the success of waking and keeping dry sheets.

Effectiveness

- Random waking – no better than spontaneous recovery (Young, 1964; Baker, 1969; McConaghy, 1969).
- Scheduled waking – no research has assessed this procedure independently.
- Staggered waking – only 'moderate' success has been documented (Creer and Davis, 1975).
- Intensive waking – assessed along with scheduled waking as a component of dry bed training, the waking procedure plus alarm proved as effective as the complete dry bed training package. Bollard and Nettelbeck (1982) suggest all but the waking schedule (i.e. RCT, positive practice and cleanliness training) as an adjunct to the alarm can be jettisoned without reducing the effectiveness. Further, the waking schedule only minimally improves the effectiveness of the alarm on its own.

When to use

- Where alarm treatment is unacceptable to the child.
- Where alarm treatment might be potentially disruptive (e.g. residential homes, boarding school).
- To guarantee a 'one-off' dry bed.
- For a limited period to avoid dependence on the parent/carer (Doleys and Ciminero, 1976).

Self awakening

Rationale

- To *internalize* the waking response.

Description (from Schmitt, 1990)

- To practise the following sequence each night before sleep:

    - lie on the bed with eyes closed;
    - pretend it is the middle of the night;
    - imagine the bladder is full;
    - feel the bladder starting to hurt;

- imagine it is trying to wake you up;
- run to the toilet and empty the bladder.

• At the end of such practice the child might be reminded to act in this way when they need to urinate during the night.

Variations

• Azrin and Theines (1978) employed a similar strategy incorporating extra drinks and practising a self awakening strategy *when* the child indicated a need to toilet.

Effectiveness

• To date there is little published work on the effectiveness of this procedure.

When to use

• The older child.
• Children who have difficulty in waking to the alarm.

Waking by association

Rationale

• To secure the *relationship* between alarm triggering and waking.

Description (from Friman and Warzak, 1990)

• During the daytime when the child is urinating in the toilet, a parent stands outside the toilet door and triggers the alarm.
• The child should try and stop urinating as quickly as possible in response to the alarm.

Effectiveness

• The paired association procedure has yet to be evaluated but Friman and Warzak (1990) suggest it is a useful adjunct to the alarm because Oswald *et al.*'s (1960) study indicates discrimination between incoming stimuli on the basis of meaningfulness and prior training during sleep is probable.

When to use

• With children having difficulty in waking to the alarm.

Cognitions

Auto-suggestion

Rationale

• To develop *awareness* of bladder control;
• To enhance *confidence*;
• To develop a *preparedness* to wake.

Description (from Butler and Parkin, 1989)

• The child is encouraged to practise daily some meaningful self instructions/suggestions.
• These should be phrased in ways understood by the child.
• They are *cued* to particular events, such as:

    – Each time the child drinks: '*I want to be dry, I can be dry*'.
    – When involved in physical activity: '*I can control my bladder like I control other muscles*'.
    – When urinating in the toilet: '*I am boss of my bladder*'.
    – When passing a toilet door: '*I can only wee in the toilet*'.
    – When in bed, prior to sleep: '*I will wake if I need to use the toilet*'.

Variations

• Many of these auto-suggestions derive from self hypnotic procedures advocated by Gardner and Olness (1981) who also taught the child ways of relaxing.

Effectiveness

- Edwards and Van der Spuy (1985) studied the components of hypnosis – relaxation (or trance) and self instructions – and discovered the trance was not essential and the effectiveness of hypnotherapy was primarily due to the auto-suggestions.
- Using auto-suggestion in the waking state appears to reduce the frequency of bedwetting although only 19% achieved initial success criteria (Edwards and Van der Spuy, 1985).

When to use

- With the older child.
- To encourage a preparedness to wake, or respond to the alarm triggering.

Restructuring beliefs

Rationale

- To enhance *responsibility* and *control* over the achievement of dry nights.
- To develop the child's belief that he/she is active in changing his/her behaviour.

Description (from Butler, 1987)

- When success begins to emerge on any of the parameters discussed in Chapter 10 – smaller patches, waking quickly, dry nights – the child should be encouraged to *attribute this internally*.
- Internal attributions consist of a belief that the child has control over the reasons for success – a developing ability to wake, respond to bladder sensations, control the detrusor.
- It is important the child acknowledges the reasons for success are due to him/her, *not* to the alarm or parental involvement.

When to use

- Whenever success is apparent.
- To reduce dependency on 'external' factors such as the alarm.
- During withdrawal from medication (see Chapter 12).

Visualization

Rationale

- To employ *imagery* as a vehicle for establishing bladder control.

Description (from Butler 1993d)

- Introduce to the child, using pictures if necessary, the functioning of the bladder.
- Invite the child to conjure up *images* of the *processes*:

  - The bladder filling and stretching, e.g. like a balloon.
  - Reaching maximum capacity, e.g. a balloon full of water at the point of bursting.
  - Transmission of signal to the brain, e.g. red pulses flashing through nerve tunnels.
  - The brain being alerted and waking, e.g. a bell tingling in the brain.

- When the child feels happy with the images, encourage him/her to practise the process lying on the bed with eyes closed, just prior to sleep.

Effectiveness

- A case study by Butler (1993d) documented the immediate response in a boy previously dependent on the alarm to wake.

When to use

- The older child.

- To alleviate relapse following the removal of the alarm.
- With children who function well in the visual area.

Intake

Diet/fluids

Rationale

- To eliminate from the diet any food products which increase vulnerability to bedwetting.

Description

- The following products have been linked with nocturnal enuresis:

  - Dairy products and chocolate (Esperanca and Gerrard, 1969b; Egger *et al.*, 1992).
  - Citrus fruit juices, especially orange and blackcurrant (Esperanca and Gerrard, 1969b; Egger *et al.*, 1992).
  - Coffee, tea, cocoa and cola, because of the diuretic effects of such substances (Pierce, 1980).

Effectiveness

- Esperanca and Gerrard (1969b) advocated apple juice, ginger ale and water as fluid substitutes and found 25% of children achieved a substantial increase in dry beds. However, a replication by McKendry *et al.* (1975) failed to achieve such success.
- The improvements through diet appear to take the form of reduced frequency of wetting episodes rather than 'cure' (McKendry *et al.*, 1975).

Overlearning

Rationale

- To strengthen the detrusor muscles and the bladder's maximum functional capacity.
- To increase demands upon the newly acquired responses underlying nocturnal bladder control which either enables the child to demonstrate a 'margin of error' (when no further wetting episodes occur), or it affords additional learning trials (when wetting recurs).

Description (from Morgan, 1978)

- Commence overlearning following the achievement of success (14 consecutive dry nights).
- Continue employing the alarm.
- Encourage the child to increase fluid intake in the last hour before bed, up to a maximum of 1 pint.
- Continue with this increased fluid each night until a further 14 consecutive dry nights have been achieved, whereupon remove the alarm and continue with fluids as normal.
- Expect some increase in bedwetting episodes but help the child to construe these as extra learning trials.
- Where renewed wetting does occur and is not reduced after 2 weeks of extra fluid, the overlearning can be terminated and persist with the alarm for a further 14 consecutive dry nights.

Variations

- The increased fluid intake can be initiated at the onset of alarm treatment (Finley *et al.*, 1982) rather than as a consequence of reaching the dryness criteria.

Effectiveness

- An expected relapse rate of around 30% with the alarm is reduced to 10% with overlearning (Young and Morgan, 1972d, 1972e; Houts *et al.*, 1986).
- Morgan (1978) presented a survey of studies on overlearning and documented 12.8% relapse with 211 cases.

When to use

- To prevent relapse.

Incentives

Arousal training

Rationale

- To reinforce the appropriate behaviour in response to alarm triggering.

Description (from Van Londen et al., 1993)

- Following the alarm triggering the child is expected to:

  - turn off the alarm within 3 minutes;
  - go to the toilet to urinate;
  - return to bed and reset the alarm.

- For responding in such a way the child receives two stickers.
- For not responding in this way the child 'pays a debt' (of one sticker).

Effectiveness

- Van Londen *et al.* (1993) report a 98% success (14 consecutive dry nights) with 41 children within 6 weeks, which was significantly superior to alarm treatment on its own.
- Relapse with arousal training was also reported to be low with 73% of children remaining dry after 2½ years.

When to use

- Perhaps more appropriate for the younger child (7–12 years).

Rewards

Rationale

- To increase the child's motivation by reinforcing progress towards becoming dry.

Description (see Fig. 5.6)

- In discussion with the child, discover what he/she would like to *do* (e.g. eat out, hire a video, go to the cinema, go to the park, swimming, extra TV privileges)
- Choose three or four activities and encourage parents to allocate a number of points for each, depending on the financial cost to the parent.
- Select a range of behaviours appropriate to achieving bladder control and award points for each:

e.g. toileting (without prompt) before bed	1 pt
waking spontaneously to toilet	2 pts
small patch on alarm triggering	1 pt
dry night	3pts

- Encourage child and parent to keep a chart to monitor points awarded.
- Child can 'trade in' the points when he/she has achieved enough for the privilege or carry on 'saving' for the next privilege.
- Parents have to remain in control of the privileges, and honour the child's wishes when enough points have been accrued.
- Because the privileges relate to what the child would like to do, the family can also enjoy the child's choice.
- No points are ever deducted.

Variations

- With younger children, incentive charts (see Chapter 12), stars or smiling faces can be used.
- Praise the child throughout the day for the achievement and inform relatives/clinician of the child's progress (Azrin *et al.*, 1974).

- With all reward systems the following features mark a successful programme:

  - No black marks or punishment for not achieving the target.
  - All rewards should be accompanied with *praise* and *information* as to why the reward has been achieved.
  - The reward (point, star etc.) has to be given immediately following the appropriate behaviour.
  - Don't make the privilege too difficult to achieve.
  - Keep it positive.
  - Remain consistent.

Effectiveness

- Emphasis on tangible rewards may reduce the child's intrinsic pleasure in mastering bladder control (e.g. Harter, 1978) and thus when the reward is terminated the bedwetting may recur. For this reason it is important to work not for tangible rewards (things the child would like to *have*), but for things the child would wish to *do*.

When to use

- With the younger child.
- With cooperative, non-punitive parents who do not perceive the reward as a 'bribe'.

Reward and penalty

Rationale

- To reinforce improvements and attach aversive consequences to wet nights.

Description (from Kaplan et al., 1989)

- Before the first night, discuss, negotiate and agree with the child:

  - A reward for being dry (e.g. special playtime, late bedtime,

extra TV). Note that the reward is not tangible, but a readily available privilege – what the child would wish to *do*.
 – A penalty for wetting (e.g. reduced TV viewing).

• The following day the child claims the reward or forfeits the privilege depending on whether he/she was dry or wet
• The rewards and penalties are *faded*, so that the child earns a 'day off' the programme for each dry week. Thus following the first dry week, the following week will have the programme instituted on 6 days, with 1 day off. If the child is dry this week, the subsequent week will consist of 5 days on the programme and 2 off. Such fading continues until the child is entirely off the programme. Where there is a wetting episode the child repeats the week without advancing to more days off the programme until a further dry week is achieved.

Variations

• It is important the child understands the reward or penalty programme is not intended to suggest that he/she is purposefully wetting the bed.

Effectiveness

• Kaplan *et al.* (1989) found as an adjunct to the alarm that this programme reduced the relapse rate in the 6 months following success.

When to use

• With the younger child.
• Where dry nights are already occurring (so the rewards become available).
• To prevent relapse.
• With committed, positive and enthusiastic parents where the penalty is not employed as a threat or developed into a punitive reaction.

11

Medication

Children are too important to be the monopoly of doctors John Apter

Whilst alarm treatment is acknowledged as 'the treatment of choice', there are surveys, particularly in the USA, which suggest physicians remain in favour of medication as the preferred option in treating nocturnal enuresis (Shelov *et al.*, 1981; Foxman *et al.*, 1986)

Many types of medication have been suggested, but only three classes have survived as effective following vigorous evaluative trials. They appear to operate on different physiological systems and are:

- The tricyclic antidepressants (imipramine and amitriptyline), which act on the *brain* and *bladder*.
- The synthetic analogue of vasopressin (desmopressin), which influences *kidney* functioning.
- The anticholinergics (oxybutynin) which affect *bladder* functioning.

This chapter discusses the three types in relation to: mode of action, administration, effectiveness, pretreatment predictors, side effects and when to use.

Mode of action

Imipramine

According to Johnson (1980), their use was first suggested by a psychologist Hugh Esson who observed a difficulty in urination in many depressed adults who were being prescribed imipramine.

The exact pharmacological action of tricyclics in enuresis is not understood, but four mechanisms have been proposed (Miller *et al.*, 1992):

- *An antidepressant effect,* but as this takes up to 10–12 days to develop (Rapoport *et al.*, 1980) it fails to account for the immediate reduction in bedwetting which is observed when the medication is effective.
- *Alteration in arousal and sleep,* yet sleep studies fail to support an association between sleep stages and enuresis, with bedwetting occurring at any stage (Mikkelson *et al.*, 1980; Norgaard, Hansen and Neilsen, 1985).
- *An anticholinergic response* which is supported by Rushton (1989) who demonstrated an increase in bladder capacity in those treated with imipramine compared to untreated controls.
- *An increase in antidiuretic hormone* (vasopressin) which reduces urine production a view supported by the work of Puri (1980).

Desmopressin

For some time the phenomenon of reduced urine production at night compared with the day has been known. George *et al.* (1975) suggested the mediating factor was plasma vasopressin which is released in a circadian rhythm. Norgaard *et al.* (1989) found evidence for this with older enuretic children and adults showing a lack of circadian vasopressin release, resulting in a *inability to reduce urine volume at night* and an *inability to concentrate urine production at night*. Thus the child's bladder capacity is exceeded, resulting in bedwetting. What the theory fails to account for is why the child fails to wake at the point of maximum bladder capacity, because to wet the bed a child has to both overfill the bladder capacity *and* be unable to arouse from sleep to the stimulus of a full bladder (Moffatt *et al.*, 1993)

A lack of vasopressin release does not account for all children with enuresis (Holland *et al.*, 1993) and indeed there are no surveys of population samples to determine how common the pattern is.

Vasopressin appears to be released as a pulsatile fashion with a 'short life' of approximately 5–7 minutes (Holland *et al.*, 1993).

Thus to be an effective medication a long acting 'substitute' is required, and has been achieved with desmopressin which is a synthetic analogue of the antidiuretic hormone vasopressin which remains effective for 10–12 hours (Schmitt, 1990).

Oxybutynin

Miller *et al.* (1992) suggest this anticholinergic drug reduces uninhibited detrusor muscle contractors, and is therefore useful for children who have associated daytime wetting, urgency and dysfunctional detrusor symptoms.

Administration

Imipramine

- The starting dose is usually 25 mg, 1 hour before bedtime, with a maximum dosage of 50 mg for children 8–12 years and 75 mg for older children (Schmitt, 1990).
- Large doses do not increase the success rate (Schmitt, 1990).
- Usually prescribed for 3–6 months before tapering the medication over a comparable period (Poussaint and Ditman, 1982).

Desmopressin

- Desmopressin is absorbed rapidly from the nasal mucosa and is thus often prescribed as a nasal spray.
- One spray contains 10 µg of desmopressin.
- The most common dose is 20 µg which is one spray up each nostril, as late as possible in the evening after emptying the bladder (Tehro, 1991).
- Dosage may be increased to 30–40 µg.
- It must be kept refrigerated to maintain its effectiveness.
- It is odourless and tasteless.
- Desmopressin is also now available as tablet form, but the dosage is about 10 times higher than nasal spray (Fjellestad-Paulsen *et al.*, 1987).
- Since tablets are stable at room temperature they provide a flexible alternative when travelling.

- There seems no evidence of resistance to desmopressin even after long periods of treatment, nor is there antibody formation (Tehro, 1991).
- Even prolonged desmopressin administration does not appear to effect the production of endogenous vasopressin or other hormones (Rew and Rundle, 1989).
- Manufacturers suggest the child should be rested from desmopressin at 3-month intervals to assess progress without medication.

Oxybutynin

- Between 6 and 9 years, 5 mg bid.
- Between 10 and 18 years, 5 mg tid.
- After 2 months the taper should begin (Miller *et al.*, 1992).

Effectiveness

Houts *et al.* (1992) emphasize a valid point concerning studies on effectiveness – the evaluation of medication has focused on how effective it is in reducing the frequency of bedwetting, probably because the aim is to manage enuresis, whereas studies of alarm effectiveness focus on percentages of children who *reach a criteria of dryness* because the aim is to 'cure' or *alleviate* bedwetting. This makes comparison between medication and alarm studies difficult.

Imipramine

- The effect can usually be observed following the first dose (Schmitt, 1990).
- Wetting frequency can be reduced with 10–60% of children (Blackwell and Currah, 1973).
- In considerably fewer cases (of the order of 15–30%) bedwetting will be alleviated (Shaffer, 1979).
- No well controlled study reports cure rates anywhere close to 50%, and most report rates considerably lower (Johnson, 1980).
- There is no correlation between plasma concentration of imipramine and reduction of wet nights.
- It compares unfavourably with the alarm, (Wagner *et al.*,

1982) finding 83% initial success with the alarm and 33% for children using imipramine.

- Withdrawal of imipramine produces *immediate relapse* (Shaffer, 1979; Wagner *et al.*, 1982).
- Relapse continues to remain a problem despite long term use of imipramine (Shaffer, 1979).
- Gradual tapering tends to reduce the likelihood of relapse (Poussaint and Ditman, 1965; Kardash *et al.*, 1968).

Desmopressin

- Compared with imipramine it is considered the *medication of choice* in terms of effectiveness (Houts *et al.*, 1992).
- Over 450 publications on more than 12 000 patients treated with desmopressin have appeared in the last 20 years (Tehro, 1993).
- The effect of administration is immediate.
- Moffatt *et al.* (1993) reviewed 18 randomly controlled trials of desmopressin which covered 581 children. The results were:

  - Desmopressin *reduced wetting frequency* in all studies (N=14) compared with placebo.
  - 24.5% of children on desmopressin *became dry during a 2-week period* (this includes 11 studies of 326 children).

- Prolonged use of desmopressin does not increase effectiveness (Evans and Meadow, 1992).
- Stopping the desmopressin provokes immediate relapse:

  - Only 21.4% of responders maintain dryness at 12 weeks (Rittig *et al.*, 1989).
  - Only 5.7% responders maintain dryness at 6 months (Tehro, 1991; Moffatt *et al.*, 1993).

- Comparison with the alarm suggests more rapid initial response yet significantly inferior long term success for desmopressin (Wille, 1986).

Oxybutynin

- Limited success with oxybutynin is reported in children who failed imipramine (Buttarazzi, 1977).
- No success compared with placebo with enuretic children who lack detrusor instability (Lovering *et al.*, 1988).
- Some success is reported with children who have uninhibited bladder contractions (Thompson and Lauvetz, 1976).

Pre-treatment predictors

Imipramine

- More successful with the older child (Perlmutter, 1985).
- More successful with children with normal sized bladders.
- More successful with children already achieving some dry nights.

Desmopressin

- Older children respond better (Post *et al.*, 1983; Rittig *et al.*, 1989).
- More successful with children having a high morning urine osmolarity (Dimson, 1986).
- A better response with children having achieved some dry nights (Tehro *et al.*, 1984; Pedersen *et al.*, 1985; Post *et al.*, 1983).
- Worse response with secondary enuresis (Moffatt *et al.*, 1993).
- Better response with children from families where there is a family history of enuresis (Hogg and Hussman, 1993).

Side effects

Imipramine

- Anxiety, insomnia and crying (Schmitt, 1990).
- Dryness of the mouth and mood changes (Hjalmas and Sillen, 1990).
- It is potentially lethal. Imipramine is one of the most com-

mon causes of fatal poisoning through overdose in children under 5 years of age (Wiseman *et al.*, 1987). Care must be taken to keep the medicine away from children. Some older children, presumably believing in a principal that the more they take the better the result, have died from accidental overdose (Parkin and Fraser, 1972)

- Imipramine may raise the resting pulse rate and diastolic blood pressure, raising doubts that it should be prescribed for enuresis at all (Lake *et al.*, 1979).

Desmopressin

- Eight of the 18 studies surveyed by Moffatt *et al.* (1993) reported no side effects.
- Some reports have suggest headache and nasal stuffiness (Miller *et al.*, 1992) on higher doses.
- No effect on blood pressure or growth (Tehro, 1993).
- There remains the potential for water retention, given desmopressin's anti-diuretic action, and two cases of hyponatraemic convulsions have been reported, one with cystic fibrosis and the other with abundant drinking. (Bamford and Cruickshank, 1989), and excessive drinking with prescription of desmopressin should be avoided.
- The nasal absorption of desmopressin is adversely affected by colds or allergies which may be alleviated with decongestants or antihistamines. The tablet form of desmopressin may also alleviate such problems.

When to use

Imipramine

- Given the greater side effects, potential danger and inferior response rate compared with desmopressin it is hard to make a case for imipramine treatment in preference to desmopressin.
- There is potential for using imipramine where children fail with desmopressin, or as suggested by Schmitt (1990) to employ the two medications in combination with very difficult to treat children.

- When prescribed it is advocated that imipramine is kept away from young children, parents are made fully conversant with the possible dangers and the child take the medication with parental assistance.

Desmopressin

- To facilitate a rapid response in situations where drop out from treatment, adverse social circumstances or developing maternal intolerance is observed (Butler, 1993b).
- To enhance the child's confidence in being dry when sleeping away from home, and thus enable him/her to participate in social activities.
- With the older child who has failed alarm based treatment to avoid the development of emotional trauma.
- In combination with the alarm. Sukhai *et al.* (1989) found such a combination proved more effective than the alarm alone.

Oxybutynin

- Where bladder instability and daytime wetting are associated with nocturnal enuresis.

12

Monitoring progress

Why a four year old child could understand this report.
Run out and find me a four year old child. I can't make
head or tail of it. Groucho Marx

Clinicians are increasingly being encouraged to operate within a climate of evaluation. To measure, make sense of and modify. These three principles describe the central tenets of any evaluative process, whether at a micro-level relating to a child's progress in using an alarm or at a macro-level examining the impact of an enuresis service on the community at large. Evaluation, however, is only useful where it seeks to provide answers to pertinent questions. Thus assessment requires focus. This chapter describes means of assessing improvement in the following areas:

- individual progress;
- service delivery;
- service provision.

Individual progress

Measuring the child's progress in achieving bladder control customarily involves the employment of a chart, a variety of which is described and illustrated by Butler (1993c). The quality of a chart might be measured along the following parameters:

- Is it *understandable* to the child and parent? Does it make sense, and encourage them to 'interact' with it in logging details?
- Does it *inform*? Are there keys to symbols, instructions, advice, reminders of what is required?

- Does it *involve the child*? Is it age appropriate, 'user friendly', appropriate to the child's needs and invite the child to participate in filling in details of progress?
- Does it *monitor progress*? Does it provide useful and relevant data to inform child, parent and clinician about improvement?

Some useful charts will be illustrated and described.

Picture chart

Figure 12.1 illustrates one example, the clown (Butler 1993c) which might be selected where:

- the child is aged 5–7 years;
- day or night wetting is the problem.

One objective at a time should be focused on. This might be the achievement of dry nights, dry days or parts of a day, spontaneous toilet use or ability to hold. In the box the mother or child might draw something to represent a 'reward', along the lines of something he/she would wish to *do* (not have). For each success (e.g. dry night) the child colours in the shape starting with number 1, with the reward being made available for the ten completed shapes. As discussed previously, the target should be *achievable* (e.g. only select dry nights as the goal, where the child is already accomplishing some dry nights); the parent has to have *control* over the reward (e.g. the child can only accomplish the privilege by completing the ten shapes); and the reward is provided *immediately* the child completes the ten shapes. Failure to accomplish the objective (such as a wet night) is not remarked upon nor does it cause the child to 'lose' previously gained achievements.

Smiling faces

Such a chart, as illustrated in Fig. 12.2, is again useful for the younger child who already achieves some dry nights. It monitors progress over a 4-week period and has the potential to determine any patterns (e.g. whether any nights of the week prove more vulnerable for the child).

Name _____

Figure 12.1. Clown chart. Achievement of dry nights/dry days, spontaneous toilet use/ability to hold. ('In the box the mother or child might draw something to represent a 'reward' – something the child might like to do').

The child is encouraged to draw a smiling face (or place a star or sticker) when he/she achieves a dry night. A neutral face might be drawn if the child's wetting resulted in a small patch.

:) = dry

	Monday	Tuesday	Wednesday	Thursday	Friday	Saturday	Sunday
Week 1							
Week 2							
Week 3							
Week 4							

Figure 12.2. Smiling faces.

A sad face, or no drawing (leaving the choice to the child) on really wet nights will determine the extent of progress the child makes over time. Many children find completing the chart intrinsically rewarding in itself and have pleasure in bringing the chart along to the clinic for the clinician's approval. However, some privileges can also be built into the programme, whereby a number of *consecutive dry nights*, number of *cumulative* dry nights or number of *dry nights/week*, agreed prior to starting, results in a privilege (something the child would wish to do). This target when accomplished can then be gradually increased.

Progress chart

Where an alarm is being used, this type of chart proves invaluable (Butler, 1987). Illustrated in Fig. 12.3, it seeks to detail information for each night, and focuses on parameters which determine the degree of progress being made by the child. It fosters a positive attitude and enables the clinician to determine (before dry beds are achieved) whether the alarm is influencing the attainment of nocturnal bladder control. The chart covers 14 nights and provides space for important information – a contact number and the date of next appointment. As described by Butler (1987) the chart encourages the clinician to monitor the following aspects of progress:

- Number of *dry nights per week*; number of *consecutive dry nights*, which might not be expected to increase in the first few weeks.
- *Self waking*, or spontaneous waking to use the toilet, which is suggestive of the development of awareness of bladder signals.
- *Time of alarm triggering*, which if a pattern of later triggerings emerges is indicative of increased holding capacity.
- Size of *wet patch*, where smaller patches suggests the child's responsiveness to the alarm is becoming increasingly quicker.
- The child's *waking to the alarm*, because success will depend upon sensitivity and responsiveness to alarm triggering.

PROGRESS CHART

Name: . . . .

Contact no. . . . .

Next appt. . . . .

Date	Dry ✓	Self waking	Time of alarm	When alarm is triggered:		
				Woke to alarm y/n	Size of patch s/m/l	Comments

Figure 12.3. Progress chart.

BECOMING DRY – SEQUENCES OF DRY NIGHTS

Name . . . .

◹ = Dry night

▯ = wet night – begin
a new sequence
with next dry night

Dry nights														
Sequence: Date starting	1	2	3	4	5	6	7	8	9	10	11	12	13	14

Figure 12.4. Becoming dry – sequences of dry nights.

Once dry nights begin occurring with some regularity, progress can be tracked by plotting dry nights on a line graph or histogram to provide a visual display (Butler, 1993c).

Sequence chart

Figure 12.4 illustrates this chart, the purpose of which is to use in conjunction with the progress chart, for older children, to visually display increasingly longer sequences of dry nights, with the aim of enhancing motivation through feedback.

A sequence begins with a dry night, recording the date and either checking off (✔) or colouring in night 1. Subsequent dry nights occurring consecutively are checked off along the same row, increasing in line with the number of consecutive dry nights. The row is completed on the occasion of a wet night which is recorded with a dash (|).

A new row is started on the occurrence of the next dry night and completed as before, continuing the row on each subsequent dry night and finishing with a wet night. Completing a full row indicates a run of 14 consecutive dry nights, the criteria adapted to define initial success (Butler, 1991).

Daily record of important factors

This chart, completed daily and illustrated in Fig. 12.5, seeks to determine which, if any, factors might contribute to the achievement of dry nights. It is administered for a short period of time (e.g. 1 month), and employed with the older child who is interested to understand influential factors and who already achieve some dry nights but either not sufficient to reach the success criteria or who is vulnerable to relapse (Butler, 1993e). It seeks to discover any correlations or links between dry nights and the following factors:

- Mood state (feelings) – transient emotional states following life events have been associated with nocturnal enuresis (Douglas, 1973; Rutter *et al.*, 1973). Children are asked to rate themselves on self description.
- Fluid intake and frequency of toileting.
- Practice or efforts made to improve the chances of achieving a dry bed.

DAILY RECORD OF IMPORTANT FACTORS

Name: . . . .

Date: . . . .

Day No: . . . .

1. FEELINGS:

How have you felt today?

	Not at all						Very much
	1	2	3	4	5	6	7
Happy							
Friendly							
Confident							
Tired							
Worried							
Bad tempered							
Moody							
Angry							
Frightened							
Upset							
Different from others							
On my own							
Poorly							

2. FLUID INTAKE AND TOILETING

No. drinks today . . . .

Time of last drink . . . .

What was it . . . .

No. toilet visits today . . . .

Time of last toilet before bed . . . .

3. PRACTICE

Have you tried any of these today?

Holding at toilet door	Yes/No
Stop-start	Yes/No
Increasing fluids	Yes/No
Thinking positive about my control	Yes/No

And tonight before bed?

Suggesting you can wake up	Yes/No
Feeling confident about being dry	Yes/No
Seeing it in your mind's eye	Yes/No

4. BEDTIME

Time . . . .

Lights on:

Bedroom light	Y/N
Night light	Y/N
Landing light	Y/N

6. OUTCOME

DRY [＿＿＿＿]

WET – patch: small [＿＿＿＿]

medium [＿＿＿＿]

large [＿＿＿＿]

5. WAKING

____Woke to alarm

____Woke by myself and used toilet

____Woke but didn't use toilet

____Mum/Dad woke me

____Woke for other reasons

Figure 12.5. Daily record of important factors.

- Bedtime – the time, and whether lights were left on.
- Waking.
- Outcome.

Schedule of reduction

In Chapter 11 the problem of relapse following the withdrawal of medication was highlighted. A programme of structured withdrawal has been shown to significantly reduce the problem of relapse (Butler and Holland, in preparation) and the chart shown in Fig. 12.6 illustrates an 8-week programme and records the child's progress. The chart is useful for older children and:

- informs the child which nights to take medication (*) without any reduction of dosage;
- depicts the reduction of medication over 8 weeks from 4×/week to once/week;
- informs the child when *not* to take medication (blank). Often alternative interventions such as the enuresis alarm are employed on such nights;
- encourage dry nights to be monitored by shading in the appropriate sections.

Part of the success of this programme in preventing relapse is the phasing in of alternative methods, and secondly the observation and feedback of the occurrence of dry nights on *non-medication* nights. Discussion with the child of such instances enables the child to feel the dry nights were achieved through *internal* means, rather than external factors such as medication or the alarm. Internal attributions for success have been found to reduce the chance of relapse (Atthowe, 1973).

Service delivery

Monitoring the success of the service as a whole becomes important in determining future directions of the service. Two salient measures of success are:

- Effectiveness.

SCHEDULE OF REDUCTION

* Medication   Dry ◣
                 Wet ◺

Week	Day 1	Day 2	Day 3	Day 4	Day 5	Day 6	Day 7
1	*		*	*		*	
2	*	*		*			*
3		*			*		*
4	*		*			*	
5		*			*		
6		*				*	
7			*				*
8				*			

Figure 12.6. Schedule of reduction of medication.

• Consumer acceptability.

Effectiveness

This requires the collection of outcome data for a series of children treated, either over the period of a year or sample of children (e.g. the first 50 treated). Categories of outcome are outlined by Butler (1991) and may be elaborated further:

• *Initial success* (the achievement of 14 consecutive dry nights). It is possible to obtain parameters of improvement to determine the 'speed of success' – how quickly or efficiently the child achieves bladder control (Butler *et al.*, 1988; Butler *et al.*, (1990c); Gustafson, 1993):

- number of wet nights before the first dry night;
- number of nights to initial success (including the 14 consecutive dry nights);
- number of wet nights before initial success;
- number of wet nights in 16 weeks of treatment.

- *Drop out* (the failure to attend for two consecutive appointments, or treatment discontinued by agreement). Drop outs may be categorized as *unavoidable* (e.g. children moving out of the area) or *avoidable* where for example the treatment intervention was completed prematurely because the family elected not to continue with an alarm. Such cases might validly be considered failures.
- *Failure* (the failure to meet the initial success criteria within 16 weeks).

Morgan (1993) has proposed a formula for determining the percentage effectiveness of a service delivery:

$$\text{Effectiveness} = \frac{\text{No. successes}}{\text{No. children treated }*} \times 100$$

(* this is inclusive of all children whether drop out or not).

Consumer acceptability

Having a means of collating parents' and child's views of the service offered both meets the 'Guidelines on Minimum Standards of Practice', (Morgan, 1993) and enables a perceived evaluation to influence the future planning and direction of the service delivery.

Butler (1993c) provides an easily administered questionnaire for parents which seeks to determine their feelings and perceptions in the following areas:

- Pre-appointment information about the service.
- The waiting time before the first appointment.
- Efficiency at the clinic (e.g. suitable times, seen on time).
- Contact and time between appointments.

- Clinician's attitude (understanding, listening, explanations).
- Treatment interventions (appropriateness, patient's choice, effectiveness).
- Methods of monitoring progress.
- Alarm malfunctioning.
- Complaints and suggestions.

Service provision

The 'Guidelines on Minimum Standards of Practice' (Morgan, 1993) seeks to enhance the quality of service provided through a variety of processes. Enuresis services do require regular monitoring to determine how successfully they meet the criteria set out in the Guide, and to encourage decisions which constantly seek to improve the way the service is structured and delivered. The essential questions to consider in examining a service are:

- Is the service *accessible* to children with enuresis?

  - Are parents and the community served by the clinic aware of the service? Is it publicized through posters, pamphlets and notices in relevant local centres such as libraries and health centres?
  - Do the range of professionals likely to be in contact with children with enuresis know of the service and routes to referral? Such professionals might include GPs, paediatricians, urologists, nephrologists, clinical medical officers, clinical and educational psychologists, health visitors, school nurses, practice nurses, continence advisors, social services.

- Is the service *relevant to the needs* of the population?

  - does the service provide for the range of children who might wish to access the service? This might include:
    the younger child;
    ethnic minorities;
    children with learning difficulties;
    children with physical disabilities;

the older adolescent;
children with associated problems (e.g. daytime wetting, encopresis);
children living away from home (e.g. children's homes, boarding schools).

- Is the service *acceptable* to the children and parents?

  - Are children seen quickly following referral?
  - Is choice between different treatment interventions offered?
  - Are children followed up with regularity and in tune with the families needs?
  - Do children and parents have the chance to voice their opinion of the service?

- Is the service *effective*?

  - Are treatment interventions based on interventions with a proven history of effectiveness?
  - Are alarms readily available to use?
  - Are alarms returned following their use?
  - Is the percentage of children reaching the success criteria acceptable?
  - Is there an unreasonable drop out rate?
  - Are relapses kept to a minimum?

The culmination of all our efforts towards helping children gain nocturnal bladder control is the satisfied expressions of parents and the glint of enthusiasm radiating from a child who perceives himself as 'free at last'. It is apposite to end with a flavour of such fulfilment. A thoughtful and delighted mother put it across like this, 'Different types of intervention were negotiated which enabled him to explore the possibilities without pressure to fulfil certain expectations . . . . he is obviously delighted with the outcome, and he's also learnt something about his learning style.' For the child, he reflected on his achievement in this way, 'I've had a friend to stay at our house and I've stayed for 2 nights at my cousin's house. The guitar ensemble that I'm in has organized a residential weekend which I'm going on. I feel I can do so much more now'.

This was a boy who had struggled for 5 years to overcome nocturnal enuresis (Butler, 1993d). His commitment was absolute, his willingness to try new ideas undeniable and his success, when it came, unquestionably well earned. He did present a challenge but then, is that not why we choose to work in this field?

Appendix A

Enuresis alarms

1. Body worn alarms
- MDI – Mini Drinite
  N H Eastwood & Sons Ltd
  118 East Barnet Road
  Barnet, Herts EN4 8RE

  - Replaceable sensor.
  - MVI Mini Drinite is a vibrator version.

- Night Trainer
  Nottingham Rehab
  17 Ludlow Hill Road
  West Bridgford
  Nottingham NG2 6HD

  - sensor attached.
  - PCT (Personal Continence Trainer is a vibrator version).

- Goodnight
  Simcare, Eschmanm Bros &
  Walsh Ltd
  Peter Road, Lancing
  West Sussex BN15 8TJ

  - No wires attaching sensor.
  - Dual signal (audible and vibration).
  - Key to stop the alarm.

2. Bed type alarms
- Enuresis Alarm
  Headingly Scientific
  Services
  45 Westcombe Avenue
  Leeds LS8 2BS

  - A single bed pad.
  - No switches – the alarm is set by plugging in the pad.
  - Attachments: extension alarm with 6-m of connecting wire; silent wakener; extra loud alarm.

- *Astric Dry Bed*
  Astric Medical
  Astric House
  148 Lewes Road, Brighton
  Sussex BN2 3LG

- A single bed pad.
- The alarm is set by plugging in the pad.
- The bed pad can be adapted to fit other alarm boxes.

- *SMI Drinite*   N H Eastwood & Sons Ltd
                                   118 East Barnet Road
                                   Barnet, Herts EN4 8RE
- A foil track embossed plastic mat.
- Pulsed audible alarm and visible indicator on alarm box.
- Attachments: extension alarm (PEX1) with 10 m lead,
booster audible with silent awakener (PEX2); silent
vibrator awakener (PEX3); booster with loud variable
pitch (PEX4)

Appendix B

Enuresis services

1. Home treatment pack   London Enuresis Clinic
                             14 Burlington Lodge Studios
                             Buer Road
                             London SW6 4JJ

   - A body worn alarm.
   - An instructional video.
   - A detailed manual.
   - A chart to monitor progress.

2. Consultancy, literature information, newsletters
                             Enuresis Resource &
                             Information Centre
                             65 St Michael's Hill
                             Bristol BS2 8DZ

3. Training for professionals

                             Dr Richard Butler
                             Dept Clinical Psychology
                             High Royds Hospital
                             Menston, Nr Ilkley LS29 6AQ

   - Basic and advanced courses.
   - Models of service delivery.
   - Quality issues.

Appendix C

Useful products

1. Waterproof bedding
- Waterproof duvets and pillows

    Permalux Park House,
    Blackburn Road
    Birstall, Batley
    W Yorkshire WF17 9PL

- Waterproof duvets and pillows

    Feeder Products Ltd
    9 Willoughby Drive
    Chelmsford, Essex CM2 6UT

2. Protective bedding
- Mattress cover   Boots the Chemist

- Protective duvet, pillow, mattress cover and 'Terry' waterproof fitted sheet

    E.R.I.C.
    65 St Michael's Hill
    Bristol BS2 8DZ

- Protective quilt, pillow, mattress cover and sleeping bag protector

    Feeder Products Ltd
    9 Willoughby Drive
    Chelmsford, Essex CM2 6UT

- Protective quilt and pillow covers

    Orthomed Limited
    5 Loaning Road
    Edinburgh EH7 6JE

Appendix D

Available literature

1. For children and adolescents

*   Butler, R. J. and Parkin G. (1989) *Eric's Wet to Dry Bedtime Book*. Nottingham Rehab, Nottingham.
    *   For age 7+; a self help manual.
    *   Available from E.R.I.C. and Nottingham Rehab.

*   Adams, J. (1990) *You and Your Alarm*, E.R.I.C., Bristol.
    *   For age 7+, a manual to assist with the alarm.
    *   Available from E.R.I.C.

*   Dobson, P. (1991) *A Guide for Teenagers*. E.R.I.C., Bristol.
    *   Information and facts for the adolescent.
    *   Available from E.R.I.C.

2. For parents

*   Azrin, N. H. and Besalel, V. A., (1979) *A Parent's Guide to Bedwetting Control: A Step-by-Step Method*. Simon & Schuster, New York.
    *   A detailed account of dry bed training.

*   Meadow, R. (1980) *Help for Bed Wetting*. Churchill Livingstone, Edinburgh.
    *   A brief introduction.

*   Dobson, P. (1988) *Bedwetting: a Guide for Parents*. E.R.I.C., Bristol.
    *   A brief guide.

*   Adams, J. (1990) *Your Child's Alarm*. E.R.I.C., Bristol.
    *   A guide for parents in using the alarm.

- Morgan, R. (1992) *Help for the Bedwetting Child*. Credor, London.
  - A comprehensive overview.
  - Available from E.R.I.C.

3. For professionals

- Baller, W. R. (1975) *Bed-Wetting: Origins and Treatment*. Pergamon Press, New York.
  - Particular emphasis on the alarm.

- Butler, R. J. (1987) *Nocturnal Enuresis: Psychological Perspectives*. John Wright, Bristol.
  - Comprehensive overview, employing psychological models.

- Blackwell, C. (1989) *A Guide to Enuresis*. E.R.I.C., Bristol.
  - A practical handbook.

- Butler, R. J. (1992) *Nocturnal Enuresis: A Manual of Treatment Methods*. C.M.H.T., Leeds.
  - A review of the range and variety of treatment interventions.
  - Available from the author, Dept of Clinical Psychology, High Royds Hospital, Menston, Nr Ilkley LS29 6AQ.

- Morgan, R. T. T. (1993) *Guidelines on Minimum Standards of Practice in the Treatment of Enuresis*. E.R.I.C., Bristol.
  - A source book for quality statements related to the delivery of enuresis services.

- Butler, R. J. (1993) *Enuresis Resource Pack*. E.R.I.C., Bristol.
  - Charts, questionnaires, information and tips for use and photocopying.

References and further reading

American Psychiatric Association (1980) Diagnostic and Statistical Manual of Mental Disorders (3rd edn) A.P.A., Washington, D.C.

Anon (1987) My enuresis, *Arch. Dis. Child.*, **62**, 866–868.

Antaki, C. and Brewin, C. R. (1982) *Attributions and Psychological Change: Applications of Attributional Theories to Clinical and Educational Practice.* Academic Press, London.

Atthowe, J. M. (1973) Nocturnal enuresis and behaviour therapy: a functional analysis. In *Advances in Behaviour Therapy* (Vol. 4) (eds R. B. Rubin, J. Henderson, H. Fensterheim and L. P. Ullman), Academic Press, New York.

Azrin, N. H. and Theines, P. M. (1978) Rapid elimination of enuresis by intensive learning without a conditioning apparatus. *Behav. Ther.*, **9**, 342–354.

Azrin, N. H., Sneed, T. J. and Foxx, R. M. (1973) Dry-bed: a rapid method of eliminating bedwetting (enuresis) of the retarded. *Behav. Res. Ther.*, **11**, 427–434.

Azrin, N. H., Sneed, T. J. and Foxx, R. M. (1974) Dry-bed training: Rapid elimination of childhood enuresis. *Behav. Res. Ther.*, **12**, 147–156.

Baker, B. L. (1969) Symptom treatment and symptom substitution in enuresis. *J. Abnorm. Psychol.*, **74**, 42–49.

Bakwin, H. (1971) Enuresis in twins. *Am. J. Dis. Child.*, **121**, 222–225.

Baller, W. R. (1975) *Bed-Wetting: Origins and Treatment.* Pergamon Press, New York.

Bamford, M. F. M. and Cruickshank, G. (1989) Dangers of intranasal desmopressin for nocturnal enuresis. *J. R. Coll. Gen. Pract.*, **39**, 345–346.

Bannister, D. (1986) Personal communication.

Bannister, D. and Fransella, F. (1986) *Inquiring Man: The Psychology of Personal Constructs*, 3rd edn, Croom Helm, London.

Belsky J. and Vondra J. (1987) Child maltreatment: prevalence, consequences, causes and prevention. In *Childhood Aggression and Violence* (eds D. H. Crowell, I. M. Evans and C. R. O'Donnell) Plenum, New York.

Bennett, G. A., Walkden, V. J., Curtis, R. H., Burns, L. E., Rees, J., Gosling, J. A. and McQuire, N. L. (1985) Pad-and-buzzer training, dry-bed training, and Stop-start training in the treatment of primary nocturnal enuresis, *Behav. Psychother.* **13**, 309–319.

Berger, R. M., Maizels, M. and Moran, G. C. (1983) Bladder capacity (ounces) equals age (years) plus 2 predicts normal bladder capacity and aids in diagnosis of abnormal voiding patterns. *J. Urol.*, **129**, 347.

Blackwell, B. and Currah, J. (1973) The psychopharmacology of nocturnal enuresis. In *Bladder Control and Enuresis* (eds I. Kolvin, R. C. MacKeith and S. R. Meadow) Heinemann, London.

Bollard, J. (1982) A 2-year follow up of bedwetters treated by dry bed training and standard conditioning. *Behav. Res. Ther.*, **20**, 571–580.

Bollard, J. and Nettelbeck, T. (1981) A comparison of dry bed training and standard urine-alarm conditioning treatment of childhood bedwetting. *Behav. Res. Ther.*, **19**, 215–226.

Bollard, J. and Nettelbeck, T. (1982) A component analysis of dry bed training for treatment of bedwetting, *Behav. Res. Ther.*, **20**, 383–390.

Bowlby, J. (1971) *Attachment and Loss, Vol. 1. Attachment*, Penguin, Harmondsworth.

Boyd, M. M. (1960) The depth of sleep in enuretic school children and in non-enuretic controls. *J. Psychosom. Res.*, **44**, 274–281.

Brazelton, T. B. (1962) A child oriented approach to toilet training. *Paediatrics*, **29**, 121–128.

Brazelton, T. B. (1973) Is enuresis preventable? In *Bladder Control and Enuresis* (eds I. Kolvin, R. C. MacKeith and S. R. Meadow) Heinemann, London.

Breugelmans, A. L. and Wyndaele, T. (1992) Urodynamic findings in patients below 12 years old with different clinical types of enuresis. *Acta Urol. Belgica*, **60**, 65–71.

Broughton, R. J. (1968). Sleep disorders: Disorders of arousal? *Science*, **159**, 1070–1077.

Butler, R. J. (1987) *Nocturnal Enuresis: Psychological Perspectives.* John Wright & Son, Bristol.

Butler, R. J. (1991) Establishment of working definitions in nocturnal enuresis. *Arch. Dis. Child.*, **66,** 267–271.

Butler, R. J. (1992) *Nocturnal Enuresis: A Manual of Treatment Methods.* Leeds CMH Trust, Leeds.

Butler, R. J. (1993a) Maternal attitudes towards nocturnal enuresis: the implications for treatment. *Ferring Lit. Service,* **2,** 2–3.

Butler, R. J. (1993b) *How children perceive enuresis and the implications for treatment,* Presentation at IERC, Aarhus, Denmark.

Butler, R. J. (1993c) *Enuresis Resource Pack.* ERIC, Bristol.

Butler, R. J. (1993d) Establishing a dry run: a case study in securing bladder control. *Br. J. Clin. Psychol.,* **32,** 215–217.

Butler, R. J. (1993e) Monitoring influential factors in the achievement of bladder control. *Clin. Psychol. Psychother.,* **1,** 111–115.

Butler, R. J. (in prep). A randomised clinical trial of body worn alarms.

Butler, R. J. and Brewin, C. R. (1986) Maternal views of nocturnal enuresis. *Health Visitor,* **59,** 207–209.

Butler, R. J. and Holland, P. (in prep) The investigation of a structured programme of withdrawal of medication in the prevention of relapse following treatment for childhood nocturnal enuresis: a pilot study.

Butler, R. J. and Parkin, G. (1989) *Eric's Wet to Dry Bedtime Book.* Nottingham Rehab., Nottingham.

Butler, R. J. Redfern, E. J. and Holland, P. (1994) Children's notions about enuresis: and the implications for treatment. *Scand. J. Urol. Nephrol.* (in press).

Butler, R. J., Brewin, C. R. and Forsythe, W. I. (1986) Maternal attributions and tolerance for nocturnal enuresis. *Behav. Res. Ther.,* **24,** 307–312.

Butler, R. J., Brewin, C. R. and Forsythe, W. I. (1988) A comparison of two approaches to the treatment of nocturnal enuresis and the prediction of effectiveness using pre-treatment variables. *J. Child Psychol. Psychiatry,* **29,** 501–509.

Butler, R. J., Redfern, E. J. and Forsythe, W. I. (1990a) The child's construing of nocturnal enuresis: a method of enquiry and prediction of outcome. *J. Child Psychol. Psychiatry,* **31,** 447–454.

Butler, R. J., Brewin, C. R. and Forsythe, W. I. (1990b) Relapse in children treated for nocturnal enuresis: prediction of response using pre-treatment variables. *Behav. Psychother.*, **18,** 65–72.

Butler, R. J., Forsythe, W. I. and Robertson, J. (1990c) The body worn alarm in the treatment of nocturnal enuresis. *Br. J. Clin. Pract.*, **44,** 237–241.

Butler, R. J., Redfern, E. J. and Forsythe, W. I. (1993) The maternal tolerance scale and nocturnal enuresis. *Behav. Res. Ther.*, **31,** 433–436.

Butler-Sloss Lord Justice (1988) *Report of the Inquiry into Child Abuse in Cleveland 1987.* HMSO, London.

Buttarazzi, P. J. (1977) Oxybutynin chloride (ditropan) in enuresis. *J. Urol.*, **118,** 46.

Christmanson, L. and Lisper, H. O. (1982) Parent behaviours related to bedwetting and toilet training as etiological factors in primary enuresis. *Scand. J. Behav. Ther.*, **11,** 29–37.

Cohen, M. W. (1975) Enuresis. *Pediatr. Clin. North Am.*, **22,** 545–560.

Collins, R. W. (1973) Importance of the bladder-cue buzzer contingency in the conditioning treatment for enuresis. *J. Abnorm. Psychol.*, **82,** 299–308.

Collins, R. W. (1976) Applying the Mowrer conditioning device to nocturnal enuresis. *J. Pediatr. Psychol.*, **4,** 27–30.

Collins, R. W. (1980) Enuresis and encopresis. In *Encyclopedia of Clinical Assessment*, (ed. R. H. Woody), Jossey-Bass, San Francisco.

Couchells, S. M., Johnson, S. B., Carter, R. and Walker, D. (1981) Behavioural and environmental characteristics of treated and untreated enuretic children and matched nonenuretic controls. *J. Paediatr.*, **99,** 812–816.

Creer, T. and Davis, M. H. (1975) Using a staggered wakening procedure with enuretic children in an institutional setting. *J. Behav. Ther. Exp. Psychiatry*, **6,** 23–25.

Crosby, N. D. (1950) Essential enuresis: Treatment based on physiological concepts. *Med. J. Aust.*, **2,** 533–543.

De Jonge, G. A. (1973) Epidemiology of enuresis: a survey of the literature. In *Bladder Control and Enuresis*, (eds I. Kolvin, R. C. McKeith and S. R. Meadow), Heinemann, London.

DeLeon, G. and Mandell, W. (1966) A comparison of conditioning and psychotherapy in the treatment of functional enuresis. *J. Clin. Psychol.*, **22,** 326–330.

Devlin, J. B. (1991) Prevalence and risk factors for childhood nocturnal enuresis. *Irish Med. J.*, **84,** 118–120.

Devlin, J. B. and O'Cathain, C. (1990) Predicting treatment outcome in nocturnal enuresis. *Arch. Dis. Child.*, **65**, 1158–1161.

Dimson, S. B. (1986) DDAVP and urine osmolality in refractory enuresis. *Arch. Dis. Child.*, **61**, 1104–1107.

Dische, S. (1971) Management of enuresis. *Br. Med. J.*, **2**, 33–36.

Dische, S. (1973) Treatment of enuresis with an enuresis alarm. In *Bladder Control and Enuresis* (eds I. Kolvin, R. C. McKeith and S. R. Meadow), Heinemann, London.

Dische, S. (1988) Enuresis in children (letter). *Archives of Disease in Childhood*, **63**, 225–226.

Dische, S., Yule, W., Corbett, J. and Hand, D. (1983) Childhood nocturnal enuresis: factors associated with outcome of treatment with an enuresis alarm. *Dev. Med. Child Neurol.*, **25**, 67–80.

Dobson, P. (1991) *A Guide for Teenagers*, ERIC, Bristol.

Dobson, P. (1993) Literature disseminated from the Enuresis Resource & Information Centre, Bristol.

Dodge, W. F., West, E. F., Bridgforth, E. B. and Travis, L. B. (1970) Nocturnal enuresis in 6–10 year old children: Correlation with bacteriuria, proteinuria and dysuria. *Am. J. Dis. Child.*, **120**, 32–35.

Doleys, D. M. (1977) Behavioural treatments for nocturnal enuresis in children: a review of the recent literature. *Psychol. Bull.*, **84**, 30–54.

Doleys, D. M. and Ciminero, A. R. (1976) Childhood enuresis: Considerations in treatment. *J. Pediatr. Psychol.*, **4**, 21–23.

Doleys, D. M., Ciminero, A. R., Tollinson, J. W., Williams, C. L. and Wells, K. C. (1977) Dry bed training and retention control training: a comparison. *Behav. Ther.*, **8**, 541–548.

Douglas, J. W. B. (1973) Early disturbing events and later enuresis. In *Bladder Control and Enuresis*, (eds I. Kolvin, R. C. McKeith and S. R. Meadow), Heinemann, London.

Edwards, S. D. and Van Der Spuy, H. J. J. (1985) Hypnotherapy as a treatment for enuresis. *J. Child Psychol. Psychiatry*, **26**, 161–170.

Egger, J., Carter, C. H., Soothill, J. F. and Wilson, J. (1992) Effect of diet treatment on enuresis in children with migraine or hyperkinetic behaviour. *Clin. Pediatr.*, **5**, 302–307.

Esperanca, M. and Gerrard, J. W. (1969a) Nocturnal enuresis: studies in bladder function in normal children and enuretics. *Can. Med. Assoc. J.*, **101**, 324–327.

Esperanca, M. and Gerrard, J. W. (1969b) Nocturnal enuresis: Comparison of the effect of imipramine and dietary restriction on bladder capacity. *Can. Med. Assoc. J.*, **101**, 721–724.

Essen, J. and Peckham, C. (1976) Nocturnal enuresis in childhood. *Dev. Med. Child Neurol.*, **18**, 577–589.

Evans, J. H. C. and Meadow, S. R. (1992) Desmopressin in bedwetting: length of treatment, vasopressin secretion and response. *Arch. Dis. Child.*, **67**, 184–188.

Feehan, M., McGee, R., Stanton, W. and Silva, P. A. (1990) A 6-year follow up of childhood enuresis: prevalence in adolescence and consequences for mental health. *J. Pediatr. Child Health*, **26**, 75–79.

Fenichel, O. (1945) *The Psychoanalytic Theory of Neurosis*, Norton, New York.

Fergusson, D. M., Horwood, L. J. and Shannon, F. T. (1986) Factors related to the age of attainment of nocturnal bladder control: an 8-year longitudinal study. *Paediatrics*, **78**, 884–890.

Fergusson, D. M., Horwood, L. J. and Shannon, F. T. (1990) Secondary enuresis in a birth cohort of New Zealand children. *Pediatr. Perinat. Epidemiol.*, **4**, 53–63.

Fielding, D. M. (1980) The response of day and night wetting children and children who wet only at night to retention control training and the enuresis alarm. *Behav. Res. Ther.*, **18**, 305–317.

Fielding, D. M. (1982) An analysis of the behaviour of day and night wetting children: towards a model of micturition control. *Behav. Res. Ther.*, **20**, 49–60.

Fielding, D. M. (1985) Factors associated with drop out, relapse and failure in the conditioning treatment of nocturnal enuresis. *Behav. Psychother.*, **13**, 174–185.

Fielding, D. M. and Doleys, D. M. (1987) Elimination problems: Enuresis and encopresis. In *Behavioural Assessment of Childhood Disorder*, 2nd edn (eds E. J. Mash and L. G. Terdal), Guildford Press, London.

Finley, W. W., Rainwater, A. J. and Johnson, G. (1982) Effect of varying alarm schedules on acquisition and relapse parameters in the conditioning treatment of enuresis. *Behav. Res. Ther.*, **20**, 69–80.

Fitzwater, D. and Macknin, M. L. (1992) Risk/benefit ratio in enuresis therapy. *Clin. Pediatr.*, **5**, 308–310.

Fjellestad-Paulsen, A., Wille, S. and Harris, A. S. (1987) Comparison of intranasal and oral desmopressin for nocturnal enuresis. *Arch. Dis. Child.*, **62**, 674–677.

Fordham, K. E. and Meadow, S. R. (1989) Controlled trial of standard pad and bell alarm against mini alarm for nocturnal enuresis. *Arch. Dis. Child.*, **64**, 651–656.

Forrester, R. M., Stein, Z. and Susser, M. W. (1964) A trial of conditioning therapy in nocturnal enuresis. *Dev. Med. Child Neurol.*, **6**, 158–166.

Forsythe, W. I. and Butler, R. J. (1989) Fifty years of enuretic alarms. *Arch. Dis. Child.*, **64**, 879–885.

Forsythe, W. I. and Redmond, A. (1970) Enuresis and the electric alarm: Study of 200 cases. *Br. Med, J.*, **1**, 211–213.

Forsythe, W. I. and Redmond, A. (1974) Enuresis and spontaneous cure rate: study of 1129 enuretics. *Arch. Dis. Child.*, **49**, 259–263.

Foxman, B., Burciaga Valdez, R. B. and Brook, R. J. (1986) Childhood enuresis: prevalence perceived impact and prescribed treatment. *Paediatrics*, **77**, 482–487.

Freyman, R. (1963) Follow up study of enuresis treated with a bell apparatus. *J. Child Psychol. Psychiatr.*, **4**, 199–206.

Friman, P. C. and Warzak, W. J. (1990) Nocturnal enuresis: a prevalent, persistent, yet curable parasomnia. *Paediatrics*, **17**, 38–45.

Frude, N. (1991) *Understanding Family Problems: A Psychological Approach.* Wiley, Chichester.

Gardner, G. G. and Olness, K. (1981) *Hypnosis and Hypnotherapy with Children.* Grune & Stratton, New York.

Geffken, G., Johnson, S. B. and Walker, D. (1986) Behavioural interventions for childhood nocturnal enuresis: the differential effect of bladder capacity on treatment progress and outcome. *Health Psychol.*, **5**, 261–272.

George, C. P. L., Messerli, F. H., Genest, J., Nowaczynski, W., Boucher, R., Kuchel, O. and Rojo-Ortega, M. (1975) Diurnal variation of plasma vasopressin in man. *J. Clin. Endocrinol. Metab.*, **41**, 332–338.

Gillin, J. C., Rapoport, J. L., Mikkelsen, E. J., Langer, D., Vanskiver, C. and Mendelson, W. (1982) EEG sleep patterns in enuresis: a further analysis and comparison with normal controls. *Biol. Psychiatry*, **17**, 947–953.

Glicklich, L. B. (1951) An historical account of enuresis. *Pediatrics*, **8**, 859–876.

Goldstein, S. and Book, R. (1983) A functional model for the treatment of primary enuresis. *School Psychol. Rev.*, **12**, 97–101.

Gorodzinsky, F. P. (1984) Enuresis in children. *MOD. Med. Canada*, **39**, 7–9.

Gosling, J. A., Dixon, J. S., Critchley, H. O. D. and Thompson, S. A. (1981) A comparative study of the human external sphincter and periurethral levator ani muscles. *Br. J. Urol.*, **53**, 35–41.

Graham, P. (1973) Depth of sleep and enuresis: a critical review. In *Bladder Control and Enuresis*, (eds I. Kolvin, R. C. McKeith and S. R. Meadow), Heinemann, London.

Green, D. (1986) The origins of resilience, changes. *Psychol. Psychother. J.*, **4**, 276–278.

Griffiths, P., Meldrum, C. and McWilliam, R. (1982) Dry bed training in the treatment of nocturnal enuresis in childhood: a research report. *J. Child Psychol. Psychiatry*, **23**, 485–495.

Gustafson, R. (1993) Conditioning treatment of children's bedwetting: a follow up and predictive study. *Psychol. Rep.*, **72**, 923–930.

Haque, M., Ellerstein, N. S., Gundy, J. H., Shelov, S. P. and Weiss, J. C. (1981) Parental perceptions of enuresis: a collaborative study. *Am. J. Dis. Child.*, **135**, 809–811.

Harris, L. S. and Purohit, A. P. (1977) Bladder training and enuresis: a controlled trial. *Behav. Res. Ther.*, **15**, 485–490.

Harter, S. (1978) Pleasure derived from challenge and the effects of receiving grades on children's difficulty level choices. *Child Dev.*, **49**, 788–799.

Hjalmas, K. and Sillen, U. (1990) Pharmacological treatment of bedwetting. *Drug Invest.*, **2**, [suppl. 5], 17–21.

Hladky, S. B. and Rink, T. J. (1986) *Body Fluid and Kidney Physiology*, Edward Arnold, London.

Hogg, R. J. and Hussman, D. (1993) The role of family history in predicting response to desmopressin in nocturnal enuresis. *J. Urol.*, **150**, 444–445.

Holland, P., Wood, C. M. and Butler, R. J. (1993) Nocturnal enuresis: a unifying hypothesis. (Paper presented at IERC conference, Aarhus, Denmark.)

Houts, A. C. (1991) Nocturnal enuresis as a biobehavioural problem. *Behav. Ther.*, **22**, 133–151.

Houts, A. C. and Liebert, R. M. (1984) *Bedwetting: a Guide for Parents and Children*, Charles C. Thomas, Springfield.

Houts, A. C., Peterson, J. K. and Whelan, J. P. (1986) Prevention of relapse in Full-spectrum home training for primary enuresis: a component analysis. *Behav. Ther.*, **17**, 462–469.

Houts, A. C., Berman, J. S. and Abramson, H. (1992) *The effectiveness of Psychological and Pharmacological Treatments for Nocturnal Enuresis*, manuscript from Memphis State University.

Imhof, B. (1956) Bettnasser in der erziehungsberatung. *Heilpadag., Werkbl.*, **25**, 122–127.

Jarvelin, M. R. (1989) Developmental history and neurological findings in enuretic children. *Dev. Med. Child Neurol.*, **31**, 728–736.

Jarvelin, M. R., Vikevainen-Tervonen, L., Moilanen, I. and Huttunen, N. P. (1988) Enuresis in seven year old children. *Acta Paediatr. Scand.*, **77**, 148–153.

Jarvelin, M. R., Moilanen, I., Vikevainen-Tervonen, L. and Huttunen, N. P. (1990) Life changes and protective capacities in enuretic and non-enuretic children *J. Child Psychol. Psychiatry*, **31**, 763–774.

Jarvelin, M. R., Moilanen, I., Kangas, K., Moring, K., Vikevainen-Tervonen, L., Huttunen, N. P. and Seppanen, J. (1991) Aetiological and precipitating factors for childhood enuresis. *Acta Paediatr. Scand.*, **80**, 361–369.

Jehu, D., Morgan, R. T. T., Turner, R. K. and Jones, A. (1977) A controlled trial of the treatment of nocturnal enuresis in residential homes for children. *Behav. Res. Ther.*, **15**, 1–16.

Johnson, S. B. (1980) Enuresis. In *Clinical Behaviour Therapy and Behaviour Modification*, Vol. 1, (ed. R. D Daitzman). Garland STPM Press, London.

Kales, A., Kales, J. and Jacobsen, A. (1977) Effects of imipramine on enuretic frequency and sleep stages. *Pediatrics*, **60**, 431–436.

Kaplan, H. I. and Sadock, B. J. (1982) *Modern Synopsis of Comprehensive Textbook of Psychiatry III*, Williams and Wilkins, Baltimore.

Kaplan, S. L., Breit, M., Gauthier, B. and Busner, J. (1989) A comparison of three nocturnal enuresis treatment methods. *J. Am. Acad. Child Adolesc. Psychiatry*, **28**, 282–286.

Kardash, S., Hillman, E. and Werry, J. (1968) Efficiency of imipramine in childhood enuresis: a double blind control study with placebo. *Can. Med. Assoc. J.*, **99**, 263–266.

Kelly, G. A. (1955) *The Psychology of Personal Constructs*, Vols. I & II, Norton, New York.

Klackenberg, G. (1981) Nocturnal enuresis in a longitudinal perspective. *Acta. Paediatr. Scand.*, **70**, 453–457.

Kolvin, I., Taunch, J., Currah, J., Garside, R. F., Nolan, J. and Shaw, W. B. (1972) Enuresis: a descriptive analysis and a controlled trial. *Dev. Med. Child Neurol.*, **14**, 715–726.

Lake, C. R., Mikkelsen, E. J., Rapoport, J. L., Zavadil, A. P. and Kopin, I. J. (1979) Effect of imipramine on norepinephrine and blood pressure in enuretic boys. *Clin. Pharmacol. Ther.*, **26**, 647–653.

Larrence, D. T. and Twentyman, C. T. (1983) Maternal attributions and child abuse. *J. Abnorm. Psychol.*, **92**, 449–457.

Liberman, B. L. (1978) The role of mastery in psychotherapy: Maintenance of improvement and prescriptive change. In *Effective Ingredients of Successful Psychotherapy*, (eds J. D. Frank, R. Hoehn-Saric, S. D. Imber, B. L. Liberman and A. R. Stone), Bruner & Mazel, New York.

Lovering, J. S., Tallett, S. E. and McKendry, J. B. J. (1988) Oxybutynin efficacy in the treatment of primary enuresis. *Paediatrics*, **82**, 104–106.

Lovibond, S. H. (1964) *Conditioning and Enuresis*, Pergamon Press, Oxford.

Lovibond, S. H. (1972) Critique of Turner, Young and Rachman's conditioning treatment of enuresis. *Behav. Res. Ther.*, **10**, 287–289.

Lovibond, S. H. and Coote, M. A. (1970) *Enuresis*. In *Symptoms of Psychopathology*, (ed. C. G. Costello) Wiley, New York.

Lunt, P. personal communication.

McConaghy, N. (1969) A controlled trial of imipramine, amphetamine, pad and bell conditioning and random awakening in the treatment of nocturnal enuresis. *Med. J. Aust.*, **2**, 237–239.

MacKeith, R. C., Meadow, S. R. and Turner, R. K. (1973) How children become dry. In *Bladder Control and Enuresis*, (eds. I. Kolvin, R. C. MacKeith and S. R. Meadow), Heinemann, London.

McKendry, J. B. J. and Stewart, D. A. (1974) Enuresis. *Pediatr. Clin. N. Am.*, **21**, 1019–1028.

McKendry, J. B. J., Stewart, D. A., Jeffs, R. D. and Mozes, A. (1972) Enuresis treated by an improved waking apparatus. *Can. Med. Assoc. J.*, **106**, 27–29.

McKendry, J. B. J., Stewart, D. A., Khanna, F. and Netley, C. (1975) Primary enuresis: Relative success of three methods of treatment. *Can. Med. Assoc. J.*, **113**, 953–955.

McLean, C. (1993) A personal account of enuresis. Paper presented at the 3rd annual conference of the Enuresis Resource and Information Centre Centre, Manchester.

Marshall, S., Marshall, H. H. and Lyon, R. P. (1973) Enuresis: an analysis of various therapeutic approaches. *Pediatrics*, **52**, 813–817.

Meadow, S. R. (1977) How to use buzzer alarms to cure bedwetting. *Br. Med. J.*, **2**, 1073–1075.

Meadow, S. R. (1980) *Help for Bed Wetting*, Churchill Livingstone, Edinburgh.

Meadow, S. R. (1990) Day wetting. *Pediatr. Nephrol.*, **4**, 178–184.

Mikkelson, E. J., Rapoport, J. L., Nee, L., Gruenau, C., Mendelson, W. and Gillin, L. C. (1980) Childhood enuresis: sleep patterns and psychopathology. *Arch. Gen. Psychiatry*, **37**, 1139–1144.

Miller, F. J. W. (1973) Children who wet the bed. In *Bladder Control and Enuresis*, (eds. I. Kolvin, R. C. MacKeith and S. R. Meadow), Heinemann, London.

Miller, K., Atkin, B. and Moody, M. L. (1992) Drug therapy for nocturnal enuresis: current treatment recommendations. *Drugs*, **44**, 47–56.

Moffatt, M. E. (1989) Nocturnal enuresis: psychologic implications of treatment and non-treatment. *J. Paediatr.*, **114**, 697–704.

Moffatt, M. E. (1993) The enuretic child: Is there an indication for treatment? Paper presented at IERC, Aarhus, Denmark.

Moffatt, M. E., Kato, C. and Pless, I. B. (1987) Improvements in self concept after treatment of nocturnal enuresis: randomised controlled trial. *J. Paediatr.*, **110**, 647–652.

Moffatt, M. E., Harlos, S., Kirshen, A. J. and Burd, L. (1993) Desmopressin cetate and nocturnal enuresis: how much do we know? *Paediatrics*, **92**, 420–425.

Morgan, R. T. T. (1978) Relapse and therapeutic response in the conditioning treatment of enuresis: a review of recent findings on intermittent reinforcement, overlearning and stimulus intensity, *Behav. Res. Ther.*, **16**, 273–279.

Morgan, R. T. T. (1981) *Childhood Incontinence*, Heinemann, London.

Morgan, R. T. T. (1984) Paul: bedwetting – one of the commonest problems of all. In *Behavioural Treatments with Children*, (ed. R. Morgan) Heinemann, London,.

Morgan, R. T. T. (1993) *Guidelines on Minimum Standards of Practice in the Treatment of Enuresis*, ERIC, Bristol.

Morgan, R. T. T. and Young, G. C. (1972a) The treatment of enuresis: Merits of conditioning methods. *Commun. Med.*, **128**, 119–121.

Morgan, R. T. T. and Young, G. C. (1972b) The conditioning treatment of childhood enuresis. *Br. J. Soc. Work*, **2**, 503–509.

Morgan, R. T. T. and Young, G. C. (1975) Parental attitudes and the conditioning treatment of childhood enuresis. *Behav. Res. Ther.*, **13**, 197–199.

Mowrer, O. H. and Mowrer, W. M. (1938) Enuresis: a method for its study and treatment. *Am. J. Orthopsychiatry*, **8**, 436–459.

Netley, C., Khanna, F., McKendry, J. B. J. and Lovering, J. S. (1984) Effects of different methods of treatment of primary enuresis on psychologic functioning in children. *Can. Med. Assoc. J.*, **131**, 577–579.

Nilsson, A., Almgren, P., Kohler, E. and Kohler, L. (1973) Enuresis: the importance of maternal attitudes and personality. A prospective study of pregnant women and a follow up of their children. *Acta Psychiatr. Scand.*, **49**, 114–130.

Noll, R. B. and Seagull, A. A. (1982) Beyond informed consent: ethical and philosophical considerations in using behaviour modifications or play therapy in the treatment of enuresis. *J. Clin. Child Psychol.*, **11**, 44–49.

Norgaard, J. P. (1989a) Urodynamics in enuretics: reservoir function. *Neurourol. Urodyn.*, **8**, 199–211.

Norgaard, J. P. (1989b) Urodynamics in enuretics: a pressure/flow study. *Neurourol. Urodyn.*, **8**, 213–217.

Norgaard, J. P. (1992) A pathogenesis-based approach to enuresis. *Dialog. Paediatr. Urol.*, **15**, 5–6.

Norgaard, J. P. (1993) Nocturnal enuresis: a burden on family economy. Paper presented at IERC, Aarhus, Denmark.

Norgaard, J. P., Hansen, J. M. and Neilsen, J. B. (1985) Simultaneous registration of sleep stages and bladder activity in enuresis. *Urology*, **26**, 316.

Norgaard, J. P., Pedersen, E. B. and Djurhuus, J. C. (1985) Diurnal anti-diuretic hormone levels in enuretics. *J. Urol.*, **134**, 1029–1031.

Norgaard, J. P., Rittig, S. and Djurhuus, J. C. (1989) Nocturnal enuresis: an approach to treatment based on pathogenesis. *J. Paediatr.*, **114**, 705–710.

Novello, A. C. and Novello, R. (1987) Enuresis. *Paediatr. Clin. N. Am.*, **34**, 719–733.

Oppel, W. C., Harper, P. A. and Rider, R. V. (1968a) The age of attaining bladder control. *Pediatrics*, **42**, 614–626.

Oppel, W. C., Harper, P. A. and Rider, R. V. (1968b) Social, psychological and neurological factors associated with nocturnal enuresis. *Pediatrics*, **42**, 627–641.

Oswald, K., Taylor, A. M. and Treisman, M. (1960) Discriminative responses to stimulation during human sleep. *Brain*, **83**, 440–445.

Parkin, J. M. and Fraser, M. S. (1972) Poisoning as a complication of enuresis. *Dev. Med. Child Neurol.*, **14**, 727–730.

Paschalis, A. P., Kimmel, H. D. and Kimmel, E. (1972) Further study of diurnal instrumental conditioning in the treatment of enuresis nocturna. *J. Behav. Ther. Exp. Psychiatry*, **3**, 253–256.

Pedersen, P. S., Hejl, M. and Kjoller, S. S. (1985) Desamino-*d*-arginine vasopressin in childhood nocturnal enuresis. *J. Urol.*, **133**, 65–66.

Perlmutter, A. D., (1985) Enuresis. In *Clinical Paediatric Urology*, Vol. 1. (eds P. P. Kelalis, L. R. King, and A. B. Belman), W. B. Saunders, Philadelphia, pp. 311–325.

Peterson, R. A. (1971) The natural development of nocturnal bladder control. *Dev. Med. Child Neurol.*, **13**, 730–734.

Peterson, R. A., Wright, R. L. D. and Hanlon, C. C. (1969) The effects of extending the CS-UCS interval on the effectiveness of the conditioning treatment for nocturnal enuresis. *Behav. Res. Ther.*, **7**, 351–357.

Pierce, C. M. (1980) Enuresis. In *Comprehensive Textbook of Psychiatry*, 3rd edn, (eds H. I. Kaplan, A. M. Freidman and B. J. Sadock), Williams & Wilkins, Baltimore.

Post, E. M., Richman, R. A., Blackett, P. R., Duncan, P. and

Miller, K. (1983) Desmopressin response of enuretic children: effects of age and frequency of enuresis. *Am. J. Dis. Child.*, **137**, 962–963.

Poussaint, A. F. and Ditman, K. S. (1982) A controlled trial of imipramine [tofranil] in the treatment of childhood enuresis. *J. Paediatr.*, **67**, 283–290.

Powell, G. F., Brasel, J. A., Raiti, S. and Blizzard, R. M. (1967) Emotional deprivation and growth retardation simulating idiopathic hypopituitarism. *N. Engl. J. Med.*, **276**, 1279–1283.

Pressman, M. R. (1986) Sleep and sleep disorders: an introduction. *Clin. Psychol. Rev.*, **6**, 1–9.

Protinsky, H. and Dillard, C. (1983) Enuresis: a family therapy model. *Psychother. Theory, Res. Pract.*, **20**, 81–89.

Puri, V. N. (1980) Urinary levels of antidiuretic hormone in nocturnal enuresis. *Ind. J. Paediatr.*, **17**, 675–676.

Rapoport, J. L., Mikkelsen, E. J., Zavadil, A., Nee, L. and Gruenau, C. (1980) Childhood enuresis: psychopathology, tricyclic concentration in plasma and antienuretic effect. *Arch. Gen. Psychiatry*, **37**, 1146–1152.

Ravenette, A. T. (1977) Personal construct theory: an approach to the psychological investigation of children and young people. In *New Perspectives in Personal Construct Theory*, (ed. D. Bannister), Academic Press, London.

Rew, D. and Rundle, J. (1989) An assessment of the safety of regular DDAVP therapy in primary nocturnal enuresis. *Br. J. Urol.*, **63**, 352–353.

Richman, N., Stevenson, J. and Graham, P. (1982) *Preschool to School: A Behavioural Study*. Academic Press, London.

Rittig, S., Knudsen, U. B., Norgaard, J. P., Pedersen, E. B. and Djurhuus, J. C. (1989) Abnormal diurnal rhythm of plasma vasopressin and urinary output in patients with enuresis. *Am. J. Physiol.*, **256**, 664–667.

Ritvo, E. R., Ornitz, E. M., Gottlieb, F., Poussaint, A. F., Maron, B. J., Ditman, K. S. and Blinn, K. A. (1969) Arousal and non-arousal enuretic events. *Am. J. Psychiatry*, **126**, 77–84.

Rowe, D. (1987) *Beyond Fear*, Fontana, London.

Rushton, H. G. (1989) Nocturnal enuresis: epidemiology, evaluation and currently available treatment options. *J. Paediatr.*, **114**, 691–696.

Rutter, M. (1976) *Helping Troubled Children*, Penguin, Harmondsworth.

Rutter, M., Yule, W. and Graham, P. (1973) Enuresis and behavioural deviance: some epidemiological considerations. In *Bladder Control and Enuresis*, (eds I. Kolvin, R. C. McKeith and S. R. Meadow), Heinemann, London.

Sacks, S. and DeLeon, G. (1973) Conditioning two types of enuretics. *Behav. Res. Ther.*, **11**, 653–654.

Sacks, S. and DeLeon, G. (1978) Training the disturbed enuretic. *Behav. Res. Ther.*, **16**, 296–299.

Sacks, S. and DeLeon, G. (1983) Conditioning functional enuresis: follow up after retraining. *Behav. Res. Ther.*, **21**, 693–694.

Salmon, M. A., Taylor, D. C. and Lee, D. (1973) On the EEG in enuresis. In *Bladder Control and Enuresis*, (eds I. Kolvin, R. C. McKeith and S. R. Meadow), Heinemann, London.

Savage, D. C. L., Wilson, M. I., Ross, E. M. and Fee, W. M. (1969) Asymptomatic bacteriuria in girl entrants to Dundee primary schools. *Br. Med. J* **3**, 75–80.

Schaefer, C. E. (1979) *Childhood Encopresis and Enuresis: Causes and Therapy*, Van Nostrand Reinhold, New York.

Scharf, M. B. and Jennings, S. W. (1988) Childhood enuresis: relationship to sleep, aetiology, evaluation and treatment. *Ann. Behav. Med.*, **10**, 113–120.

Schmitt, B. D. (1982) Daytime wetting [diurnal enuresis]. *Pediatr. Clin. North Am.*, **29**, 9–20.

Schmitt, B. D. (1990) Efficacy and safety of drugs available for the treatment of nocturnal enuresis. *Drug Invest.*, **2**, [suppl. 5], 9–16.

Schaffer, D. (1973) The association between enuresis and emotional disorder: a review of the literature. In *Bladder Control and Enuresis*, (eds I. Kolvin, R. C. McKeith and S. R. Meadow), Heinemann, London.

Shaffer, D. (1979) Enuresis. In *Child Psychiatry: Modern Approaches*, (eds M. Rutter and L. Hersov), Blackwell, Oxford.

Shaffer, D. (1980) The development of bladder control. In *Scientific Foundations of Developmental Psychiatry*, (ed. M. Rutter), Heinemann, London.

Shaffer, D., Gardner, A. and Hedge, B. (1984) Behaviour and bladder disturbance of enuretic children: a rational classification of a common disorder. *Dev. Med. Child Neurol.*, **26**, 781–792.

Shelov, S. P., McIntire, M. S., Jones, D. J. and Heagarty, M. C.

(1981) Enuresis: a contrast of attitudes of parents and physicians. *Paediatrics*, **67**, 707–710.

Smith, S. (1974) *Bedwetting: Its Cause, Effect and Remedy*, H. R. Press, Valley Stream, New York.

Sorotzkin, B. (1984) Nocturnal enuresis: current perspectives. *Clin. Psychol. Rev.*, **4**, 293–316.

Stallard, P., Sclare, I. and Harris, R. (1992) The Children Act: Implications for Clinical Psychologists. *Clin. Psychol. Forum*, **49**, 31–34.

Starfield, B. (1967) Functional bladder capacity in enuretic and non-enuretic children. *J. Pediatr.*, **70**, 777–781.

Starfield, B. and Mellits, E. D. (1968) Increase in functional bladder capacity and improvements in enuresis. *J. Pediatr.*, **72**, 483–487.

Stein, Z. A. and Susser, M. W. (1966) Nocturnal enuresis as a phenomenon of institutions. *Dev. Med. Child Neurol.*, **8**, 677–685.

Stein, Z. A. and Susser, M. W. (1967a) Social factors in the development of sphincter control. *Dev. Med. Child Neurol.*, **9**, 692–706.

Stein, Z. A. and Susser, M. W. (1967b) The social dimensions of a symptom: a socio-medical study of enuresis. *Soc. Sci. Med.*, **1**, 183–201.

Stewart, M. A. (1975) Treatment of bedwetting. *J. Am. Med. Assoc.*, **232**, 281–283.

Strauss, M. A. and Gelles, R. J. (1986) Societal change and family violence from 1975 to 1985 as revealed by two national surveys. *J. Marriage Family*, **48**, 445–479.

Stromgren, A. and Thomsen, P. H. (1990) Personality traits in young adults with a history of conditioning treated childhood enuresis. *Acta Psychiatr. Scand.*, **81**, 538–541.

Sukhai, R. N., Mol, J. and Harris, A. S. (1989) Combined therapy of enuresis alarm and desmopressin in the treatment of nocturnal enuresis. *Eur. J. Paediatr.*, **148**, 465–467.

Swithenbank, L. V., Carr, J. C. and Abrams, P. H. (1993) Longitudinal study of urinary symptoms and incontinence in local school children. Paper presented at IERC, Aarhus, Denmark.

Taylor, P. D. and Turner, R. K. (1975) A clinical trial of continuous, intermittent and overlearning 'bell and pad' treatments for nocturnal enuresis. *Behav. Res. Ther.*, **13**, 281–293.

Tehro, P. (1991) Desmopressin in nocturnal enuresis. *J. Urol.*, **145**, 818–820.

Tehro, P. (1993) Desmopressin in the treatment of nocturnal enuresis in children. *Ferring Lit. Search*, **2**, 2–4.

Tehro, P. and Kekomaki, M. (1984) Management of nocturnal enuresis with a vasopressin analogue. *J. Urol.*, **131**, 925–927.

Thompson, I. M. and Lauvetz, R. (1976) Oxybutynin in bladder spasm, neurogenic bladder and enuresis. *Urology*, **8**, 452–454.

Tissier, G. (1983) Bedwetting at 5 years of age. *Health Visitor*, **56**, 333–335.

Troup, C. W. and Hodgson, N. B. (1971) Nocturnal functional bladder capacity in enuretic children. *J. Urol.*, **105**, 129–132.

Turner, R. K. (1973) Conditioning treatment of nocturnal enuresis. In *Bladder Control and Enuresis*, (eds I. Kolvin, R. C. McKeith and S. R. Meadow), Heinemann, London.

Turner, R. K. and Taylor, P. (1974) Conditioning treatment of nocturnal enuresis in adults: preliminary findings. *Behav. Res. Ther.*, **12**, 41–52.

Turner, R. K., Young, G. C. and Rachman, S. (1970) Treatment of nocturnal enuresis by conditioning techniques. *Behav. Res. Ther.*, **8**, 367–381.

Van Londen, A., Van Londen Barentsen, M. W. M., Van Son, M. J. M. and Mulder, G. A. L. A. (1993) Arousal training for children suffering from nocturnal enuresis: a 2½ year follow up. *Behav. Res. Ther.*, **31**, 613–615.

Varni, J. W. (1983) Urinary and fecal incontinence. In *Clinical Behavioural Paediatrics*, (ed. J. W. Varni), Pergamon Press, Oxford.

Verhulst, F. C., Van der Lee, J. H., Akkerhuis, G. W., Sanders-Woudstra, J. A. R., Timmer, F. C. and Donkhorst, I. D. (1985) The prevalence if nocturnal enuresis: Do DSM III criteria need to be changed? *J. Child Psychol. Psychiatry*, **26**, 989–993.

Vis Melsen, V. D. (1992) Urodynamics in enuretic children. *Clin. Nucl. Med.*, **17**, 200–205.

Wagner, W. G. and Geffken, G. (1986) Enuretic children: how they view their wetting behaviour. *Child Study J.*, **16**, 13–18.

Wagner, W. G. and Hicks-Jimenez, K. (1986) Clinician's knowledge and attitudes regarding the treatment of childhood nocturnal enuresis. *Behav. Ther.*, **4**, 77–78.

Wagner, W. G. and Johnson, J. T. (1988) Childhood nocturnal enuresis: the prediction of premature withdrawal from behavioural conditioning. *J. Abnor. Child Psychol.*, **16**, 687–692.

Wagner, W. G. and Matthews, R. (1985) The treatment of nocturnal enuresis: a controlled comparison of two models of urine alarm. *Dev. Behav. Pediatr.*, **6**, 22–26.

Wagner, W. G., Johnson, S. B., Walker, D., Carter, R. and Wittner, J. (1982) A controlled comparison of two treatments for nocturnal enuresis. *J. Pediatr.*, **101**, 302–307.

Wagner, W. G., Smith, D. and Norris, W. R. (1988) The psychological adjustment of enuretic children: a comparison of two types. *J. Paediatr. Psychol.*, **13**, 33–38.

Warady, B. A., Alon, U. and Hellerstein, S. (1991) Primary nocturnal enuresis: current concepts about an old problem. *Paediatr. Ann.*, **20**, 246–255.

Weider, D. J. and Hauri, P. J. (1985) Nocturnal enuresis in children with upper airway obstruction. *Int. J. Paediatr. Otorhinolaryngol.*, **9**, 173–182.

Weir, K. (1982) Night and day wetting among a population of three year olds. *Dev. Med. Child Neurol.*, **24**, 479–484.

Werry, J. S. (1967a) Enuresis – a psychosomatic entity? *Can. Med. Assoc. J.*, **97**, 319–327.

Werry, J. S. (1967b) Nocturnal enuresis. *Med. Times*, **95**, 985–991.

Werry, J. S. and Cohrssen, J. (1965) Enuresis: an etiological and therapeutic study. *J. Pediatr.*, **67**, 423–431.

White, M. (1971) A thousand consecutive cases of enuresis: results of treatment. *Child Family*, **10**, 198–209.

Whiteside, C. G. and Arnold, E. P. (1975) Persistent primary enuresis: a urodynamic assessment. *Br. Med. J*, **1**, 364–367.

Wille, S. (1986) Comparison of desmopressin and enuresis alarm for nocturnal enuresis. *Arch. Dis. Child.*, **61**, 30–33.

Winnicott, D. W. (1953) Transitional objects and transitional phenomena. *Int. J. Psychoanal.* **34**, 89–97.

Wiseman, H. M., Guest, K., Murray, V. S. G. and Volans, G. N. (1987) Accidental poisoning in childhood: a multi centre survey. *Hum. Toxicol.*, **6**, 303–314.

Wood, C. M., Holland, P. C., Butler, R. J. and Penney, M. D. (1994) Pulsatile release of arginine vasopressin [AVP] and its effect on response to desmopressin in enuresis. *Scand. J. Urol. Nephrol.*, (in press).

Woolnough, L. (1991) Paternal and maternal attitudes towards nocturnal enuresis. Presented at 2nd Annual Conference of ERIC, Nottingham.

Wright, L. and Craig, S. (1974) A comparative study of amphetamine, ephedrine-atropine mixture, placebo, and behavioural conditioning in the treatment of nocturnal enuresis. *J. Oklahoma State Med. Assoc.*, **67**, 430–433.

Yates, A. J. (1975) *Theory and Practice in Behaviour Therapy*, Wiley, New York.

Young, G. C. (1964) A 'staggered-wakening' procedure in the treatment of enuresis. *The Medical Officer*, **111**, 142–143.

Young, G. C. (1965) Personality factors and the treatment of enuresis. *Behav. Res. Ther.*, **3**, 103–105.

Young, G. C. and Morgan, R. T. T. (1972a) Childhood enuresis: Termination of treatment by patients. *Commun. Med.*, **129**, 247–250.

Young, G. C. and Morgan, R. T. T. (1972b) Reasons for appointment failure among enuretic patients. *Commun. Med.*, **129**, 23–25.

Young, G. C. and Morgan, R. T. T. (1972c) Non-attending enuretic children. *Commun. Med.*, **127**, 158–159.

Young, G. C. and Morgan, R. T. T. (1972d) Overlearning in the conditioning treatment of enuresis. *Behav. Res. Ther.*, **10**, 147–151.

Young, G. C. and Morgan, R. T. T. (1972e) Overlearning in the conditioning treatment of enuresis: a long term follow up study. *Behav. Res. Ther.*, **10**, 419–420.

Young, G. C. and Morgan, R. T. T. (1973a) Rapidity of response to the treatment of enuresis. *Dev. Med. Child Neurol.*, **15**, 488–496.

Young, G. C. and Morgan, R. T. T. (1973b) Conditioning techniques and enuresis. *Med. J. Aust.*, **2**, 329–332.

Young, G. C. and Morgan, R. T. T. (1973c) Conditioning treatment of enuresis: Auditory intensity. *Behav. Res. Ther.*, **11**, 411–416.

Young, G. C. and Morgan, R. T. T. (1973d) Analysis of factors associated with the extinction of a conditioned response. *Behav. Res. Ther.*, **11**, 219–222.

Zaleski, A., Gerrard, J. W. and Shokier, M. H. K. (1973) Nocturnal enuresis: the importance of a small bladder capacity. In *Bladder Control and Enuresis*, (eds I. Kolvin, R. C. McKeith and S. R. Meadow), Heinemann, London.

Index